College

COLLEGE
The Female Essentials

Lakisha Henderson

authorHOUSE®

AuthorHouse™
1663 Liberty Drive
Bloomington, IN 47403
www.authorhouse.com
Phone: 1-800-839-8640

First published by AuthorHouse   11/23/2009

ISBN: 978-1-4389-7525-2 (e)
ISBN: 978-1-4389-7524-5 (sc)

Printed in the United States of America
Bloomington, Indiana

This book is printed on acid-free paper.

To my nearest and dearest, the ones
I keep close to my heart;
Thanks for being apart of my journey.

TABLE OF CONTENTS

INTRODUCTION

Dear Ladies,

Listen up, I know you may have seen survival college guide books before but have you ever found one that pertained to you. Well, this is that book! This book should show you how to navigate successfully through college and hopefully save you a future heartbreak. I hope to show you the ins and outs of your first year of college and keep you fabulous all at the same time! The next four years (or more depending on if you plan on making this whole college thing into your career) of your life will be filled with many learning experiences. Hopefully after reading this book your college experience will be heavy on the awesome times and light on the bumps and bruising. Please don't take my words too lightly because trust me, I have been there and done that and I feel as though I can tell you a few things about your future college adventure. I hope you ladies are ready because the next four years of your life can possibly be some of the best years of your life. Keep it FAB!!!

Lakisha Henderson

LIFE BEFORE COLLEGE

*T*his is the time where you are still in high school and you are daydreaming in class about your future breathtaking college experience. Before you can bring those daydreams to life you will need to decide on where you want to apply to college. Depending on what college you choose to attend may play a role in your breathtaking experience because if the college you choose isn't the right one for you, your college experience might be horrific? When deciding on a college you should factor in the majors offered, affordability, and location.

If you have dreams of being a fashion designer, what sense would it make for you to go to a school that focuses primarily on medical careers? You should focus on the programs offered in your degree of choice that can help you cultivate your natural talent. Some colleges are known for having the best engineering program or the best journalism program; just research the internet to see what college has the best program that best suits you. Check on the college website and see what classes are offered pertaining to your major of choice. This will let you know whether of not that school is the right one for you academically.

Affordability is another factor that should be detrimental in determining what school you choose to attend. If you plan on going to college and graduating with $80,000 worth of student loans, you should choose a major that you know can pay off those student loans easily during your post-graduation years. Basically, if you know you want to be a doctor, going to a college with a high tuition isn't bad; but going to that same college with dreams of being a leech living on your parent's couch will not foot the bill.

Location might also play a role in deciding what college you want to attend. If you soaked up the Florida sun all of your life, you must consider if you really want to trade in your bikini for some snow boots so you can attend a college in North Dakota. For some of you that are stuck at the hip to your family, you might not want to go to college too far because the whole homesick thing is going to be a beast for you.

Once you have weighed all of your options and you have narrowed your college choices to your top five you should seriously consider going on campus tours. Visiting your college of choice's website and taking a virtual tour does not count. Those virtual tours tend to photoshop the realness of a college campus. When you do go on campus tours make sure you ask a lot of questions and absorb your surroundings. If you see that there are current students complaining about the school, you should think if you want to be those same people with those same complaints your freshman year. Go to as many college tours as you can and check the scenery to see what college campus makes you feel comfortable.

<u>ORIENTATION</u>

After you have been accepted and committed to a college you should be invited to an orientation. Orientation is a chance for you to get more acquainted with the college, build school spirit, possibly take placement tests, get your college identification card, and register for classes. This is a time where you will meet other first year students who are probably as frightened as you. Colleges handle orientations in different ways; however, they are generally run by current college students that attend the school.

During my friend's orientation she was a contestant in a dating show and she also attended a talent show. The orientation for the first college I attended was an overnight orientation. All of the students there for the orientation were broken down into smaller groups. We made up songs about the college and while we were in the cafeteria the different groups would sing their school spirited song. I, for one, was not into all of this so I pretty much skipped out on the whole singing bit. Needless to say, my bonding experience with my fellow freshmen during this orientation wasn't the best. After I covered the basics (placement tests and class registration) I left and hung out with my best friend because she was going through an orientation at a nearby college.

I do not recommend that you leave your orientation before it's over because orientation is the best way to meet new people. At the time I hadn't cocooned into a social butterfly so I left the orientation to avoid the awkwardness of hanging out with complete strangers all day. The second orientation I went to, after I transferred to another college, was perfect for me. It lasted only one day and it was pretty much straight to the point. We took our placement test, registered for classes, took a tour of the campus, played a couple of games, ate, and left.

BEFORE YOUR FINAL FAREWELL

Another thing you should do before you start school is contact your future roommate because they will probably be your roommate for the next eight months of your life. You should get your roommates contact information through e-mail or mail. When you contact your roommate you might want to take this time to get to know her, but maybe not in a BFF kind of way. You should see where she is from, accept her as your friend on Facebook and see if the two of you have any similar interests.

After you and your new roomie have come to the realization that the two of you are die hard fans of Tyra Banks and Oprah Winfrey, you all might want to decide on who will bring the major appliances. There is no point in having two televisions and two miniature refrigerators to put into your minuscule dorm room. Before you and your new roomie go through your appliances checklist you might want to see what is prohibited in your dorm. Sorry ladies, some colleges don't allow appliances that have the possibility to set the dorm on fire (i.e. personal heaters, indoor grills, etc).

One last thing to do before you leave to go to college is dedicate some portion of your summer to say "farewell" to all your high school buds. This is a great time to just hang out and have the last little bit of fun before you embark on your college experience. Before you leave, if possible, rent out a local venue (or neighborhood club house) or beg your parents to let you borrow the basement and throw a going away party for all of your friends. If that is out of your budget, make it a point to have all of your high school friends meet up somewhere, like a local restaurant or theme park, to savor in the sweetness of high school memories.

Wishful Thinking.....

- If you and your friend from high school decide that you two want to be roommates, make sure you make mention of that when you apply for campus housing.

- Apply to as many colleges as you would like, you would rather have more choices than be stuck with the college that is two steps away from your parent's house.

- Start applying for scholarships early because it's free money. Scholarships are yours for the taking as long as you apply and get them. I suggest you visit websites dedicated to college scholarships and visit your school counselor for information pertaining to scholarships.

- Since applying for scholarships can be time consuming you should create a timeline for how many scholarship applications you want to have done in a given time (two weeks) and stick to this goal. This will allow you to pace yourself so you will not feel so overwhelmed.

- If your GPA is not the best make sure you have a great college entry letter, if required, and work with your literature teacher to work out the kinks.

- Build a good relationship with your teachers, counselors, and faculty since you will probably need them to write your letter of recommendation for college.

MOVING IN AND
THINGS TO BRING

I know you have seen the movies where a college student is moving her things in her dorm room and she is wearing a cute summer dress and five minutes and three boxes later she is done moving in all of her things. Well scratch that idea out of your head because the move in process is long and quite frankly, to me, it sucked. You will definitely want to wear comfortable clothes and make sure that whatever you wear you don't mind perspiring in. Unless you have Botox injections in your sweat glands, you may bust one mean sweat. Just imagine the summer heat, your family, you, and boxes full of your stuff in the trunk of a car waiting to be transported by hand to your dorm room.

Before you can move anything into your dorm room you may have to register yourself at your dorm building to get your dorm room number, your dorm key, and other paper work. If your dorm provides student parking (and you have already applied for on-campus student parking) at this time you may get your student parking decal and your parking space number if needed. One of the documents you might be given requires you to inspect your dorm room for any major flaws you see before you move in. Take this document seriously because if you don't notice that big tear in the carpet of your dorm room before you move in, you might be fined for it when you move out.

The atmosphere on move in day is a busy hustle of people trying to move their belongings into their closet size dorms. It can be a very crowded process and may take hours to actually get everything into your dorm room. Some colleges may provide big roll-able bins for you to put your things in and you can just catch the elevator up to your dorm floor. Other traditional older dorms may not necessarily be equipped with elevators and such, so this process of moving in may take more time and be a tad bit more difficult. So, for those of you moving your stuff to the fourth floor of a dorm building that has no elevators, have fun with that whole moving in thing.

You might want to invest in a hand trolley so it can make transporting heavy boxes a bit easier. You can get boxes from a moving company or you can ask for free boxes from your local grocery store because boxes are better for moving in than jumbo plastic bags. When using boxes make sure you label them; therefore, when you start unpacking you will know which box to start with. I would advise you to wake up at the crack of dawn and get an early start to your move in process. This way you can get a great parking spot under a shaded tree right by the entrance of your dorm building, or just a decent parking spot in general. If early is not your thing, just go to the registration table during the day and move your stuff into your dorm later on in the evening when the sun is going down. It will probably be less crowded during the latter part of the evening and the weather might be somewhat cooler.

TRADITIONAL DORMS

A traditional dorm consists of one room, two beds, and a few more furnishings (provided by the school) that can fit into your dorm room.

With the whole roommate thing, the person who gets there last doesn't really have a say so in which bed they get. Would you really wait around for someone you don't even know to show up so the two of you can play "rock, paper, scissors" for the bed next to the window? Your best bet is to get there early and if you don't do anything else, just put your bed sheets, covers, and pillows on the bed you want and leave. Hey, maybe even throw in a box or two so it looks like you put forth the effort to start the move in process.

APARTMENT STYLE HOUSING

If you are moving into an apartment style dorm you will need to provide more of your own furnishings. You will need to bring your own shower curtain, a shower rug, and personal kitchen utensils. Even though you might be sharing the kitchen with three other females you still need to bring your own set of pots and pans. You will be mad if someone burns one of your pans because they do not know how to cook. You might also want to consider bringing a lamp for your room, just so you can have more than one lighting option for your dorm room. Basically, when you are packing just think of the things you would need if you were moving into an apartment that already has furniture. Also, don't forget the fact that you have your own room so take advantage of it and pack things that will let you get creative so you can give it your personal touch.

THINGS NOT TO FORGET TO PACK

Regardless of your living situation there are some things that you just absolutely need and might forget when packing. You need to make sure you pack some feminine products because you do not want your menstrual cycle to come and remind you that you forgot to pack some pads. Also, do not forget to pack some medicine like cough syrup, cold relief, headache relief, and menstrual relief. Do not forget your first aid kit; don't wait until you burn your neck with your curling iron for you to remember that you forgot to pack some band-aids and ointment.

There are some extra items you may want to consider packing, they are not a necessity but they might make dorm room living a tad bit more comfortable. You never know the lay-out of your dorm room so just to make sure you can plug in your ceramic flat iron on your side of the room, it would be imperative that you bring an extension cord. A floor rug is something that you might want to consider if your dorm room has tile floor because I doubt that tile will be heated in the winter. There is nothing worse than getting out of a warm and cozy bed and stepping onto a frosty tile floor in the morning. Ladies, I know this might sound vain but you might want to consider bringing a full length mirror. How else are you going to see how your clothes look on you from head-to-toe? Also, don't forget to bring your hair dryer or your blow dryer…all hair types may not be able to handle the air dry route.

I know that you might have seen commercials and print ads for incoming college freshmen that advertise all the cool new gadgets and what-nots for dorm rooms. Don't get it twisted; all of the stuff that you see in those advertisements will not fit in your closet of a dorm room. So, you might want to hold off on those purchases until you know they are needed and can fit in your dorm room.

DIGITAL REALM

One thing I think is imperative to academic success is access to a computer, so you might want to consider investing in one. Just about every college campus should have a computer lab of some sort either on campus or in your dorm building. So for those of you that might not be able to budget in a computer, you will still have the ability to get your school work done and check your Facebook from time to time.

When buying a computer you might want to consider getting a laptop. One main reason is that it takes up less space than a desktop computer on your desk. Trust me when I say you will notice the lack of space when you have your big plasma screen of a monitor, a long keyboard, a pair of speakers, a mouse, and a mouse pad all fighting for space on your desk. If you decide to purchase a laptop you can take it to class with you and take notes and it's easier to transport when moving into your dorm. I can't say the same thing for those desktop computers, I personally didn't like lugging my monitor, cords, keyboard, hard drive, and speakers into my dorm and then setting it up….that process was never fun.

Another thing to consider investing in is a good printer. Schools usually provide this service, although typically with a cost per page. There are some printers that also serve as a copier, hey the more functions the better. Instead of copying your classmates notes by hand, you can copy it with your copier. One thing that you will find is a college must-have is a portable USB Jump Drive. They are life savers when presenting Power Points in class and a great back up if you just happen to forget to bring your seven page essay to class; you can just print that paper in the computer lab on the way to class.

*W*hen moving in you do not want to overstuff your dorm room with things that are unnecessary and will not be used throughout the semester. Pack smart, the better you pack the least amount of trips you should make from your dorm room to the family car. Make sure you keep a positive attitude because technically your family and friends do not have to help you move in all of your stuff and I doubt that they are getting paid to help. Lastly, after you move into your dorm make a list of the things you need or may have forgotten and pass that note to your family.

Things to remember...

- Label your boxes so when you are unpacking you will know what you are unpacking.
- Wear comfortable clothing and shoes; you are moving into a dorm room not walking down the runway.
- Claim your bed by the window before your roommate; if you are not first...you're last.
- Do not forget to pack a first-aid kit, a medicine kit, a menstrual kit, and a hair kit.
- Bring storage organizers and storage bins since your dorm room furnishings may be scarce.
- In regards to parking on most college campuses, you can not just park your car anywhere you see fit; especially if there are assigned spaces. You should know that the campus police do issue out parking tickets, the campus police will call and have someone put a boot on your car, and the campus police will call and have your car towed.
- When packing your things to move into your dorm, pack your clothes in storage bins. If you are not comfortable with storing your designer clothes in a plastic storage bin, store them in a chest that has a lock. In all honesty, you never know if your roommate has theft like tendencies.
- When packing your clothes for the whole move in process you might want to consider bringing seasonal clothing. For instance, when you first get to college you might not need that North Face Insulated Jacket that you packed. You can probably hold off on that until you go home later in the semester for Thanksgiving break.

DORM LIFE

*N*ow ladies, I know that some of you may cringe at the thought of sharing your personal space with a girl that you've never met in life. Well, if it helps you sleep better at night; just think of your new living arrangement as an extended slumber party. Whether you like it or not you will be giving up the privacy that you may have treasured while in high school and have to learn how to cope with other people's needs. For some of you, your roommate will become your new BFF and for others of you this roommate will be the sister you wished your parents would have put up for adoption. Regardless of the situation you will have to suck it up and act like you love it or at least be able to deal with it.

RESIDENT ASSISTANT

To help you settle in and get comfortable living with a complete stranger is a Resident Assistant (RA). These people are typically upperclassmen or graduate students who are probably getting a discount on housing to live in a dorm and keep order. The RA's generally have their own life and are typically good people if you get to know them. Make sure you get to know your RA because they may overlook that prohibited mini refrigerator you have hidden under your bed. No matter how your living arrangement is set up in your dorm building, you will probably have an RA.

TRADITIONAL DORMS

Many universities have different living arrangements for incoming freshmen. The typical living arrangement is a dorm that sleeps two individuals uncomfortably and may include two beds, an armoire, a dresser, and two desks. How you and your roommate decide to rearrange the dorm room may make it seem a bit more spacious. My freshman year of college my roommate and I tried to rearrange our beds in so many different ways to make our dorm room appear more spacious. It seemed that no matter how many times we tried, our beds were still an arm's length from each other. Therefore, we decided to just place our beds in the bunk bed position. This was fine by us because I had the top bunk and she had the bottom bunk. Her bed turned into the couch whenever more than two visitors came into our dorm room since there was nowhere else to sit. Living on the top bunk can be a hassle at times because climbing up and down of that bunk is no joke at night in the dark.

For those of you that will be living in a traditional dorm room with a roommate; try to be extra mindful of your roommate. Even if your roommate and you are not destined for the "Best Friends' Forever" club you should at least maintain a certain level of respect for each other. It really makes no sense to bicker with the one person that has access to your stuff in the dorm. Nobody wants to study while their roommate is watching television, and you sure don't want to type a paper while your roommate and her boyfriend are spending quality time together.

During my freshman year, my roommate and I would just make mention that we were expecting company. If I knew she was having company come over, I would just go to another one of my friend's room or find something to occupy my time and vice versa. On a side note, some colleges have visitation hours for same sex freshman dorms, so your new boo may only be able to visit you from 6:00 p.m. until 11:00 p.m. (Not the exact times but you get the drift; guest can not spend the night).

APARTMENT STYLE HOUSING

In apartment style housing there may be a kitchen, a living room, and guys that live across the hall. This type of living can be the ultimate sense of freedom as there may be no visitation hours for guy visitors since they live in the building. Please don't see this as a time to let your inner wild child run free, but see this as a time to make responsible decisions.

Even though you may have your own room, you still have to be mindful of your roommates. There are times when problems arise with the radio or the television being played too loud while a roommate is studying. I'm going to need you to know that the walls separating you from your roommate are not that thick; therefore, you might want to take that volume down a couple of notches.

With apartment style housing you might want to set up rules for the food in the refrigerator. For instance, you may be in class and begin to crave the lemon meringue pie that you had leftover from your date last night. Now wouldn't it suck if you opened up the refrigerator just to find that one of your roommates decided to enjoy the savoring taste of that pie? With this being said, you and your roommates may want to decide that whatever one buys, one eats. Therefore there is no confusion as to who ate up all of your cereal... you did. When it comes to the dishes and cleaning; whatever mess one makes, that person needs to clean it up or wash it up. Nobody wants to go to college to play mama and clean after people.

Dear Keesh,

My roommate is filthy, she is a nice girl but she is straight nasty when it comes to her cleaning habits. She doesn't clean her side of the dorm room and the stench is affecting my side of the dorm. There is only so much air freshener I can spray before I pull out some bleach and wipe the whole dorm room down. I'm a non-confrontational person and I need a way to communicate my problem with her without offending her.

Sincerely,
-Grimy Roommate Blues

I think the best way to tell your roommate that she might want to pick up a broom from time to time; is to write it in a letter. If you don't feel comfortable speaking to her verbally, write it out on paper in a nice way therefore she can not interrupt you from getting your point across. Mention to her that you are not mad at her, but you just wish she would be more considerate about you and throw away that piece of cheese pizza that has been molding on top of her desk for the past two weeks. No matter the message you want to convey to your roomie; just make sure you say it in a respectful manner and I am pretty sure the two of you will come to an understanding. If the two of you don't come to an understanding and she keeps up her filthy habits, tell your resident assistant that your roommate stinks, cross your fingers, and wish on a falling star that you get another roommate.

-Keesh

There are some things I recommend that you consider to make your roommate situation less stressful. Get to know each other's class schedule because chances are slim that the two of you are going to have the same class schedule. So when your roommate is in class and you are lying around in the dorm, take this time of silence to study for an exam, work on your paper, or dance around in your underwear. Try to get to know your roommate on a more social level, invite her to events on campus that you are interested in. You never know the two of you might be into the same sorts of things. I know it may seem bizarre to have a stranger in your personal living space all the time, so if this bothers you become active in campus organizations. Therefore, you have a reason not to be cramped up in your dorm room with your weird roommate.

THE COMMUNAL BATHROOMS

On top of getting used to your roommate some of you are going to have to adjust to communal bathrooms. Some communal bathrooms are separated by floors and some are shared amongst two or more dorm rooms. At first this whole communal bathroom thing is going to feel creepy, because if you had to share a bathroom it was probably only with one or two other siblings. These bathrooms usually have enough shower stalls, sinks, and toilets to go around so that you are not waiting in a line to use them.

Ladies, make sure you buy some beach flip flops to wear as shower shoes. Just because you share a bathroom with fifteen other females doesn't mean you have to share their feet fungus also. You should invest in a shower toting case of some sort to make it easier to keep all your stuff together while you are in the bathroom. These dorms typically provide toilet tissue for your use, but if you prefer toilet tissue with a softer touch you might want to buy your own. If you find that you are going to be spending a considerable amount of time on the toilet because those enchiladas are not holding in your stomach too well; make sure you bring air freshener. I don't think anyone wants to smell your natural funk no more than you.

Some of you ladies will not have to adjust to communal bathrooms because you will be staying in apartment style housing. You might share a bathroom with one person or multiple persons' but not so many where your bathroom becomes a communal bathroom. With this type of arrangement you might be responsible for providing your own toilet tissue. You and your roommate could either purchase your own toilet tissue or you and your roommate can switch up on who purchases toilet tissue when it runs out.

*D*orm life is a great experience and I recommend that you stay on campus your freshman year. This is a way for you to get the complete campus feel; you will be surprised how some college campuses become alive during the start of an athletic season or during homecoming week. The best way to soak in all of this college goodness is to live in a dorm on campus. A lot of your first college friends might be the girls that live on your hall or somewhere in your dorm.

I know you might be leery at the thought of living with a complete stranger, but living with a complete stranger allows you to learn how to be more understanding of other people. It can help you learn how to compromise and communicate effectively. This is a time for you to learn how to be more open-minded about people of a different background, social class, and sometimes of a different sexual orientation. Please don't think that just because your roommate is a lesbian you are going to get a free pass to a new roommate. That is technically not a reason to get a new roommate, unless you are being sexually harassed. While you are living in the dorm you might as well make it home because girlie it will be your home for the next eight months or so.

Don't Forget…

- Shower shoes; green fungus growing on your feet has never been a good look.
- Keep an open line of communication with your roommate and respect each other's space.
- Get to know your RA; they may overlook the banned items lurking in your dorm room.
- Give your dorm room, or your side of the dorm room, a personal touch when decorating.
- Eat your own food, unless your roommate is super cool and doesn't mind you eating all of her food.
- If your roommate is expecting a male guest, make sure to get lost for a couple hours…three's company.
- Invest in a portable media player of some sort so that you can play your music as loud as you want; if you are wearing earphones of course.

COLLEGE COOKING & WASHING

O nce in college you may find that you need to learn how to cook. I don't mean that you will need to become a gourmet chef overnight, but you might need to know how to make a couple of basic meals so that you don't wither away due to starvation. I knew how to cook coming into college, but because I can live off of cereal and restaurant left-over's; there wasn't much of a need for me in the kitchen. If you are like me this whole cooking thing will be a synch because as far as personal cooking, there isn't much to make because you can get full off of simple meals. A mesquite turkey sandwich, chips, applesauce, and a glass a water counts as a meal in my book. When I was really hungry I would just go out to eat, and most likely I would have left-over's and that would just become my lunch for the next day. Now, if that isn't simple I don't know what is.

Some of you might have an inner culinary chef waiting to break loose. You probably can't wait to open up those spices and get to seasoning meats and so forth. If this is you then, by all means, get your Emeril Lagasse on.....BAM! There are those of you that are kitchen impaired, you might want to stick with foods that take little to no cooking preparation. These types of meals consist of food that requires you to preheat the oven, place food on a cooking sheet, bake, and wait. This type of meal may also require you to place food on a skillet, stir occasionally, and wait. Even though you may not be cooking meals from scratch, become familiar with spices. Spices can change the taste of food you didn't prepare by hand. If you are making canned vegetables, just dab some seasoning salt in it and people will think you made it from scratch....yeah right!

When it comes to cooking, cook what you feel comfortable making and always remember to never get too preoccupied with other stuff while you are cooking; catching your dorm on fire is never a good look. On a side note, don't go grocery shopping on an empty stomach because you might bring home food that you would have never considered eating and you may notice a larger than expected grocery receipt. When you go grocery shopping on an empty stomach just about everything looks delicious which means that just about everything will be in your grocery cart. So for you cooks out there that have beginners skills you might want to consider making a grocery list before going to the grocery store.

Dear Keesh,

I am not an experienced cook by any means; while I was in high school the only time I spent in the kitchen was to eat the meals my mom made. I am terrified about grocery shopping because I don't know where to start and what to buy to complete a meal. What should I do?

Sincerely,
-Hungry Novice Cook

When grocery shopping, I recommend that you make a list of items to buy. When I go grocery shopping I think of a meal as an outfit. If I know I want to cook spaghetti, I know that I need something to go with it....like salad and toast. For instance, if you buy a dress, you need some heels and accessories to wear with it. Try buying food that has left-over potential; like meals that typically feed four people. If it's just you eating the food, you will have food for a couple of days. The frozen aisle will be your aisle of choice, because it takes little to no preparation to bake food in the oven or stir-fry on top of the oven. Also, throw some fruits and veggies in your grocery buggy and some Cranberry juice to keep you regular.

-Keesh

Since some of you ladies are unaware of how to turn on an oven, I have taken the time to give you ten easy recipes that should save you from starvation. Hopefully, these recipes are easy for you to manage and will be a great meal that you and friends can enjoy.

Mac and Cheese con Fiesta

1 box of mac and cheese

1 lb of ground beef

1 jar of salsa

Cook the ground beef until it is brown (no pink spots), drain ground beef after cooking. Cook the mac and cheese as it states on the box. Pour the mac and cheese into the ground beef. Mix the mac and cheese and ground beef together, add salsa.

Breakfast Burrito

2 tortillas   4 strips of bacon

2 eggs   1 cup of salsa

Shredded cheese

Scramble eggs to your liking and cook bacon strips (turkey bacon heats up great in the microwave). Once bacon is cooked, break the bacon into small pieces. Place flour tortillas in microwave to soften them up. Put scrambled eggs, shredded cheese, and pieces of bacon in flour tortillas and roll or fold to your liking. You can either add the salsa into your breakfast burrito or you can use it as a dipping sauce for your burrito.

Chilli con Corn Chips

1 can of chili with beans

1 bag of corn chips

Shredded cheese

Put the can of chili with beans into a pot and let it cook until done. Add shredded cheese to the pot of chili and allow the cheese to melt evenly. Grab a bowl and put a layer of corn chips in the bottom of the bowl. Add a layer of chili on top of the corn chips and if you like additional cheese, sprinkle some shredded cheese on top of the chili.

Tuna Melt

1 can of tuna	1 tablespoon of mustard
2 tablespoons of mayonnaise	1 slice of cheese
2 tablespoons of relish	2 slices of bread

Mix tuna, mayonnaise, relish, and mustard in a bowl. You will want to taste the tuna as you are mixing so you can see if you need to add any more of those ingredients. Put bread in toaster and allow the bread to toast lightly. After your bread is toasted, place the slice of cheese and tuna in between bread slices. Now you have a tuna melt.

Simple Spaghetti

1 lb of ground beef   croissant or garlic bread

1 box of spaghetti

1 can of spaghetti meat sauce

Boil water in a pot and put spaghetti in a pot until it softens up, do not leave the spaghetti in there too long because your spaghetti will be sticky. Heat up croissant or garlic bread in the oven, make sure you do not forget that it's in the oven or it will be burned and inedible. Cook ground beef until it is brown (no pink in the middle), after you have cooked the ground beef; drain it. After you drain the ground beef, add spaghetti meat sauce to the ground beef and stir. Once your spaghetti finishes boiling, let the spaghetti cool down. Put spaghetti and ground beef on a plate with your croissant or garlic bread and enjoy.

Pizza Muffins

2 English muffins

1 can of pizza sauce

Shredded cheese (mozzarella or three cheese blend)

Put the pizza sauce into microwave until heated. If you prefer your English muffins toasted you can toast them in the toaster, if not you can place them in the microwave to soften them up a bit. Once the pizza sauce is heated to your liking; place sauce on English muffins and sprinkle on an ample amount of shredded cheese. Place English muffins in microwave so that the cheese can melt, wait for it to cool down before eating. You can add pepperoni, pineapples, or other toppings to your muffin pizza.

Chicken Quesadilla

Flour tortillas

Chicken breast cut into pieces

Shredded three-cheese blend

Sour cream or salsa

Place flour tortillas in the microwave to soften up. Cut your chicken breast (after being cooked) into small pieces. After you warm your tortillas in the microwave, place shredded cheese and small chicken pieces on top. Fold your tortilla in half and heat in the microwave, cut folded tortilla into slices. You can put a dollop of sour cream on top of the tortilla after it has cooled and use the salsa for dipping.

Ramon Noodles with veggies

Pack of Ramon Noodles (works with any flavor packet you choose but the Oriental flavor works great)

Veggies of choice

Place Ramon noodles into a pot of boiling water and let cook until noodles soften. Do not overcook the noodles or they will be too sticky and may not taste as good. After the noodles have cooked, drain noodles if preferred. Add flavor packet to the noodles. Cook the veggies of choice, once cooked put veggies and Ramon noodles into a bowl and eat.

Beenie Weenies with Grilled Cheese Sandwich

1 can of barbeque flavored pork and beans

2 bread slices

Butter

2 hotdogs

Brown sugar

1 slice of cheese

Place the pork and beans into a pot and let cook. Place hotdogs in a separate pot with water and cook. After the beans finish cooking, add a dab of brown sugar. You can add more brown sugar if the pork and beans are not sweet enough for you. After the hotdogs are done, cut them into pieces and place them into the pot full of pork and beans and stir. To make the grilled cheese sandwich, take out a skillet pan and spray the pan with non-stick cooking spray. Place a dab of butter on the bread and place the grilled cheese sandwich (with cheese in-between slices) on the skillet and cook until the cheese has melted.

Chicken Caesar Salad

Caesar salad   Salad dressing of choice (preferably Caesar dressing)

Grilled chicken strips

Shredded provolone cheese

Place chicken strips on skillet and cook. After the chicken strips are cooked, prepare your salad in a bowl or on a plate. Place chicken strips on the salad, add shredded provolone cheese and Caesar dressing.

Fruit Dip

1 cup of fruit flavored yogurt

Whipped Cream

Empty out the fruit flavored yogurt in a bowl and add whipped cream. Mix both together and now you have a dipping sauce for your fruit; add just enough whipped cream until the dipping sauce is to your liking. Get your favorite fruit, dip, and be merry!

WASHING CLOTHES 101

Since you are gaining this new found independence with living on your own there is one thing I must mention, as minuscule as it may seem; you have to know how to wash your clothes! Most dorms have a laundry facility somewhere either on campus or in the dorm building. These laundry facilities might not be busy early in the morning during the week or late at night during the week. The weekends are typically the worst time to decide to wash clothes because half of the people that live in your dorm might have chosen that same timeframe to wash their clothes.

When using these laundry facilities, I recommend that you keep track on how long each load is running. If you know that it's going to take 35 minutes for your load of clothes to finish washing; be in the laundry room in 34 minutes so you can get your clothes out of the washer and put them in the dryer without someone stealing them in the process. Please do not be one of those people that leave their clothes in the dryer for hours after they are dry. If this is you, please consider your clothes stolen because someone may come by and empty out the dryer that your clothes are in and I doubt they are going to fold your clothes for you; unless they are folding your clothes in their room to put in their dresser. You should know that people do steal and could basically care less that they stole the sweater your grandmother made for you that took her eleven months to sew. For those of you that are illiterate when it comes to washing clothes, here are a couple of pointers:

- Separate your clothes into different piles; white, dark, and bright colored clothing. You really don't want your pink skinny jeans to bleed onto every white garment you own while in the washing machine. Also wash towels separately, they tend to be linty and you will probably cry when you see your black sweater decorated with lint balls. Also, go through your jeans pockets and empty them before washing.

- Choose the water temperature for washing your clothes. Some garments have instructions for temperature settings on a care label, for those garments follow the instructions. You should wash dark colors and bright colors in warm/cold water and wash whites in hot water. If you are "Going Green" and conserving energy, just wash all of your clothes in cold water.

- Measure the amount of detergent (liquid or powder) that is needed for your load of dirty clothes. The top of the detergent bottle doubles up as a measuring cup for the liquid detergent and powder detergent usually has a scooper inside of it that is used for measuring. After you put the detergent in the washing machine put your clothes in there and start the cycle.

- Before you place your clothes in the dryer, remove the lint from the lint tray in the dryer. After you do this, place your clothes in the dryer and put a sheet of fabric softener in there. For those of you with long arms, you might want to skip this whole drying stage with your cotton long sleeved shirts. Instead, just let them air dry to prevent that most dreaded sleeve shrinkage. Anything that you fear might shrink; let it air dry. The same thing goes for jeans, let them air dry if you don't want them to become capri pants over the course of an hour.

- After you take your dry clothes out of the dryer, fold them, and continue on with your day.

*H*opefully, I've given you some advice so that you will be able to function sans your parents. This is going to be a trial and error part of your life and you will mess up and learn from your mistakes. You novice cooks are going to burn many of toasts before you get it just right and you illiterate washers are going to soil your clothes (by leaving them in the washer too long) at least once. Just in case you end up soiling your clothes, re-wash them before putting them in the dryer unless you want to walk around smelling like spoiled milk all day. Overtime, you will see that you are fully capable of feeding yourself and keeping clean clothes.

ARE MY PANTS SHRINKING?

*L*adies, I am here to tell you that the "Freshman 15" is not an urban myth. It is real and it can really sneak up on you and have your family looking at you sideways when you come home for the summer break. Everybody's body is different and everybody's metabolism is not the same. With that said; everybody can not routinely eat a couple slices of pizza with cheese bread (or something of equivalence) and take a power nap and think that they will not eventually wake up with thunder thighs. For some of you ladies, this is the time of your life where you learn what a gym is and how all of those "machines" work in there.

This new weight that you can not seem to shake off can be due to your new lifestyle of eating and sleeping during the middle of the day. In high school you might have eaten lunch around twelve or one and sometime in between then you might have had P.E. or walked up a few steps to get to class during the course of a seven hour school day. After school you were probably an active member of a sports team or at least had to walk home from the bus stop. I will give you a glance of a typical day of college from a student who is on board the train to gain the "Freshman 15." I present you with a day in the college life of Lola.

"Lola wakes up around 9:00 a.m. and gets ready for class so that she can be there by 10:00 a.m. Before she leaves her dorm room she heats up a toaster pastry and grabs a bottle of water (gotta keep that skin glowing). She catches the shuttle to get to her class building and then she rides the elevator to the seventh floor to get to her classroom. After that class she rides the elevator down to the second floor for her next class. After her classes are over by 1:00 p.m. she goes to the cafeteria and eats and talks to her friends. Once she finishes her meal of a cheeseburger, fries, chicken nuggets with a diet soda to drink; she gets tapped on the shoulder by Mr. Sleepy who informs her that she is tired. She then goes to her dorm room to take a nap and wakes up just in time to watch a re-run of her favorite reality show."

Now, unless Lola has plans to go to the gym later on in the day she is going to have a problem. Throughout the course of her short academic day Lola did not take advantage of working out. If she was going to ride the elevator to the seventh floor she could have at least walked down to the second floor and shook some of that cellulite off her legs. All she can expect at the end of her freshman year is good grades in all of her classes and fifteen more pounds to introduce to her family and friends when she goes home for summer break. If you ever find yourself doing the, "my pants are too tight dance" while putting on your pants you might want to activate that gym membership to your college's recreation facility. You might as well, seeing as how you are paying for it through your college tuition.

The on-campus dining can be different depending on what college you attend. Some colleges have the all you can eat buffet feel, these are dangerous because when you are really hungry your eyes tend to be bigger than your stomach; then over the course of the semester your stomach will catch up. With this kind of dining experience just get what you know a regular meal exist of, just because there are five different meal choices doesn't mean that you have to taste them all. Make sure you throw some vegetables in the mix too, don't forget about those greens. Some campus cafeterias don't have a buffet but they have a mixture of different meals with some local fast food chains thrown in the mix.

You might want to avoid the cafeteria around the typical 12:00 p.m. lunch hour because you might end up in long lines and it may be difficult to find somewhere to sit. If you attend college in the city, skip the college cafeteria sometime and venture out in the city and try different downtown eateries or the cafeterias inside of big business buildings. Some of these eateries give discounts to college students if you show them your student I.D. card. Regardless on how the dining situation at your college is, make sure you maintain a healthy diet and drink at least one bottle or glass of water a day.

*B*asically, don't neglect your health and your well-being. Whatever your body type may be always know that, "A Healthy Body is a Beautiful Body." Your healthy may not be a size two and for some of you your healthy is a size two but no matter what your natural body type is, love it and know that it is marvelous. If quite naturally you have more hips than a little bit, embrace it and make it work for you. College is an awkward stage in your life because you are discovering yourself as a woman. The last thing you need is to have issues with your body type while going through this phase of discovery.

10 Ways to avoid the "Freshman 15"...

1. Exercise at least twice a week but more days is preferred (or at least attempt to speed walk to class every now and then).
2. Take a physical course like volleyball or tennis for class credit.
3. Take the steps versus the elevator.
4. Avoid late night runs out to eat, that food will run straight to your hips.

5. Get your much needed rest.
6. Bring healthy snacks with you to class to get you through the day.
7. Avoid frequenting the vending machines too much in between classes.
8. Acknowledge the Food Pyramid when dining in the school's cafeteria.
9. Place snacks like chips in a smaller bag to avoid over eating and eating the whole bag of chips in one sitting.
10. Once again, drink water.

EMBRACE NEW SURROUNDINGS

*D*epending on where you attend school might play a big role on how you embrace your new surroundings. Regardless of where you go to college, you should make it a point to explore the area. This may be easier said than done if your school makes up majority of the towns population. If this is your case, make sure you broaden your horizon when exploring and check out the closest city with a mall or at least traffic lights.

For those of you attending a school in a rural area, you might have to dig deep when trying to find local hot spots. You should visit the downtown area and check out some of their local shops. The local shops might not be much compared to Neiman Marcus, but hey, it's something. You might be able to make use out of the hand woven gloves one of the local shops specializes in; at least your hands will be warm in the winter. Another thing for you ladies going to school in a small town should do is make sure you check out their eateries. Small towns usually have that one local eatery that is legend for something. You might find yourself in a town that is known for serving the biggest cheeseburger known to man, well; make room in your belly and chow down. If you can't find anything of substance to do in your college's town, ask the locals.

For those of you attending college in a big city you might find that your exploration may be a bit more interesting and sometimes more costly. You should definitely check out the historical sites because big cities tend to have some interesting history. These historical sites could shed some realism to historical events you may have learned about in high school. Also try going to museums, aquariums, and amusement parks if possible.

This could be a great time exploring the city with your friends or a great time canoodling with that hot guy in your history class while watching a beluga whale swim at the local aquarium. Try stepping outside of your comfort zone and putting those years of writing to use and sign up to share one of your poems at the café during a spoken word session. I know you may dread public speaking, but you haven't been writing poetry since you were nine years old for nothing. Maybe you can try taking a salsa class, a belly dancing class or consider going rock climbing. Some schools offer these kinds of activities and they are typically free, because you pay tuition for a reason.

BE OPEN TO OTHER CULTURES

You should take the time to embrace different cultures so you can enlighten yourself. There are many ways to culture yourself; many cities tend to have celebrations or festivals for the many cultures that are represented. You might not be apart of the heritage represented at the festival but still go and learn something. Hey, if you see a cute guy at one of the festivals, talk to him so you can be international in the dating game.

There has been an annual Festival Peachtree Latino in Downtown Atlanta, and my friend and I went even though neither one of us are of Hispanic descent. We just thought we would try to put our years of

Spanish classes to the test and see how well we could keep a conversation rolling. I tried to order food in Spanish which resulted in the guy behind the counter getting someone that was fluent in English to assist me. Let's just say, I have no idea what I was doing in my Spanish classes because my Español was rusty to say the least.

Speaking of food, another way to culture your self is through your sense of taste. The closest thing some of you have had to a cultural meal is shrimp fried rice and an egg roll with a side of chicken wings. When you get to college you should try to go to different cultural restaurants. Don't limit yourself to dining out at American chain restaurants and ordering chicken fingers; you are not a five year old child. I suggest that you take a step away from your normal eating habits and eat at cultural restaurants with some of your friends to get a taste of other cultures. You can eat sushi at a Japanese restaurant, wat and tibs at an Ethiopian restaurant, or a roti at a Jamaican restaurant. Basically, what I am saying is try new things because you would be surprise as to how great other cultural food might taste....it's like a party in your mouth waiting to happen!

STUDY ABROAD

If you want to take your cultural experience to a whole other level, you might want to consider studying abroad. Studying abroad can be a worthwhile experience that you should consider doing at least once during your college matriculation. You can choose your host country by credit requirements or by location. I think that it's awesome to travel and experience cultural norms outside of what you are used to. I'm pretty sure you will not feel like a tourist in your host country as the weeks go by. I know you might not want to miss out on things that might happen on campus, but traveling outside of the country is so much more fun than being in your cramped dorm room with a roommate that gets on your nerves.

The study abroad experience can be life changing because it can possibly open up your views culturally. When you come back from studying abroad your friends might think you are a different person because your perspective on life has been broadened due to your cultural experience. You may become more grounded because for once you might see just how fortunate you really are and you might stop dwelling on your lack of material wealth. You might even notice a change in your level of confidence because you may see just how strong of a person you are when you are away in a foreign land and out of your comfort zone. There's no running home to your family when you are thousands of miles away; you better adapt to the culture and mind your manners. Studying abroad can open the doors to long lasting friendships and create memories that are immeasurable to your experiences on campus.

Try filling in this list of things you want to do while in college (go horse back riding, do a walk for charity, study abroad, volunteer, etc) and see how many of those things you can get accomplished during your freshman year.

My list of things to do during college...

1 _____

2 _____

3 _____

4 _____

5 _____

6 _____

7 _____

8 _____

9 _____

10 _____

NEW IMAGE, NEW STYLE, NEW YOU

ollege is the perfect time to reinvent yourself if you had a hard time in high school. There may not be people from your old high school attending college with you, so you can see this whole reinventing yourself as an experiment of sorts. When I say the word "reinvent" I do not mean to change yourself to point where people don't recognize you. Let's say that you were the shy, quiet type in high school and had a membership with the chess club, Spanish club, and the "I eat my lunch alone in the library club." Once you set foot on your college campus nobody may know that you were that invisible kid in high school, so now you have the chance to let out the vivacious person that was buried inside of you.

You may not have been the invisible kid, but you were probably the person that was scared to get involved in some of the things at your school because you were afraid of what your friends would say. When you get to college you can be active and let the inner you come out. You might have been a dancer all of your life but feared joining your high school's dance team because, quite frankly, they were a bore. When you get to college, try out for the college dance team so you can put all that money your parents spent on your dance lessons to good use.

While in college you can be whatever type of person you wanted to be while you were in high school. Let's say that you had aspirations of running for class president while you were in high school, but you pretty much knew that you didn't stand a chance in winning. Well, in college you do stand a chance at winning because nobody has any preconceived notions about you and you can win the title of freshman class president based off of your confidence.

This new college image may come with a new sense of fashion. No longer are the days of you wearing pants that aren't flattering, unless you're into that whole saggy booty, hip pockets look. This might have been your look in high school because your parents controlled what clothes you wore. Maybe your choice of fashion was out of your parent's monthly financial budget. Some parents can't fathom the idea of spending over one-hundred plus dollars on a pair of designer jeans... imagine that? They would probably see those big-faced hundreds as grocery money or at least money for the monthly gas bill. With this being said, you were probably limited to what you wore during high school.

In high school, you might have feared being adventurous with your fashion game. You might have been scared of what your friends would say and didn't want to commit social suicide by being labeled "the strange kid." So with this fear, you might have stayed within the fashion norms of your high school and participated in every fashion fad. If deep down you saw yourself as a trendsetter while you were in high school, let your inner fashionista out in college!

When creating a look, play around with colors, prints, and textures. Also, play around with fingernail polishes to enhance your look. What you must come to understand is that fashion is what you make it out to be. Wear what makes you feel fabulous and comfortable no matter what people think about your attire; however, some of you may fall into one of the following categories of dress. I have compiled a brief description of the style of dress you don't want to stay in and ways to improve your look so that you can graduate from this look. Some of you may not fall into any of these three categories, but I still suggest that you read the following:

PLAIN JANE

Plain Jane's have a more simple style of dress which consists of solid colored tops and jeans; hey, they might throw a skirt in the mix at times. On a cold day, you can catch a Plain Jane wearing a slightly oversized pull-over fleece, some slightly saggy jeans, and some sneakers. Basically, Plain Jane's may choose comfort over fashion and it pretty much shows because they look a little too comfortable…and not fashionable.

WHAT TO DO: Exchange your loose pair of Plain Jane jeans for a slightly snug pair, skinny jeans, that aren't too uncomfortable but might get you a few stares while you are doing your usual in the library. You can trade in that boring oversized Plain Jane t-shit with an A-line top or a bohemian inspired top and try adding accessories into the mix. You will be surprised as to how accessories can spruce up simple attire. With accessories try ear rings, necklaces, rings, and bracelets with some color; hey, even a colored scarf would be great. But, be aware that you must not wear all of your accessories at once. If your earrings are really big and funky skip out on wearing a busy necklace.

TRENDY TRINA

If you fall into this category, you probably wear all of the latest trends and never skip a beat. When gladiator sandals were the hottest thing out, you probably had like three pair in a different color and style. You may also find that due to your habitual trendy ways, you are not always able to wear your clothes after a year because they are no longer trendy. With this need for the latest fashion, you may find that your bank account isn't looking as fashionable…insufficient funds has not and will not be a fashion trend.

WHAT TO DO: As far as following every trend, I say march to your own fashion beat. Don't make it a habit of letting fashion magazines dictate what clothes you wear; however, if you just have to follow the trends, try not to dwindle your bank account in the process. Whenever a fashion trend comes about, the high-end stores will carry it and so will the lower-end stores. You need to jet set your way to the lower-end stores; why spend $250 on snakeskin gladiator sandals when you can purchase some gladiator sandals at a more reasonable price? It makes no sense to over-extend your finances for something you probably won't wear for years to come.

NO CLOTHES NORAH

When walking throughout campus, you may see a female and think to yourself, "Now she know she needs to go home and change clothes." This is the expression for the females that fit the description of the No Clothes Norah's. They tend to wear their club attire to class as if there is an after-party after their Chemistry class. Do not be fooled by thinking that just because you are not wearing club attire to class that you are not in this category; basically, wearing anything that makes your professor excuse you from class due to your lack of clothes puts you in this category.

WHAT TO DO: Basically, abide by the rules you had when attending high school. If you didn't attend a traditional high school with a dress code please keep the following in mind: Your professor wants to teach you and not your private parts, so put some clothes on so you can keep those well hidden.

SHOPPING WITH NO INCOME

Now that you are in college you have control over your bank account, which means you have some control over what you wear. But don't forget that you are a fashionista on a fixed income or in better words….a budget. You will come to understand that your college years may be your financially unstable years and having to file for bankruptcy because of your slight addiction to high-end fashion is not a good look. It may seem hard to be financially unstable and fabulous, but I am here to tell you that it's not that hard. There are many ways to shop on a college refund check budget; although it may take a little bit more navigating through sales racks and putting different garment pieces together to keep up that oh so FAB look.

During this time of frugalness stores like Forever 21 and H&M will be your best friends. These stores have a lot of clothes that look nice and also fit your budget. You also might want to look into the women's department in Target; don't sleep on Target because hot designers have been able to head up their women's collection. These garments are fashionable and will definitely fit into your college income. For you designer chicks that can not seem to live without your Antik Denim Jeans or your Marc Jacobs dresses. You might want to consider sample sales at your favorite boutique. Most boutiques have an annual sample sale where they pretty much sale off clothes that did not sale when they were on the sales floor. These items are typically forty-five percent or more off of retail price, so there are great deals at sample sales. If sample sales are out of your budget but you still want designer things you should shop at department stores like Loehmann's, Off Sak's Fifth Avenue, Marshalls, and TJ Maxx. These department stores have designer clothes that are generally less expensive than the average retail price. This can save you big bucks when you want to look like a million bucks.

I may be reaching for some of you when I mention that you should consider going to thrift stores. I personally love looking through the racks of vintage thrift stores; you will be surprised as to what pieces you can find at these places. Also, try going to thrift stores in the wealthier parts of town. Hey, the same woman that spent two hundred dollars on a skirt will drop that two hundred dollar skirt right off at the thrift store. You should be able to find some nice, gently used clothing at those thrift stores.

I'm sorry to say but when it comes to buying heels or shoes for that matter, I don't recommend cutting too many corners. Its one thing to buy some heels on sale at Nordstrom but it's another thing when you just flat out buy some cheap low quality heels. Ladies trust me, you might not feel the pain of buying those $20 (retail price) heels in your bank account, but you will surely feel that pain in your feet. Sometimes these cheap heels are made with poor quality and in the long run can have you rocking bunions and corns on your feet.

One good way to find affordable shoes is to shop at stores like DSW, Rack Room Shoes, and Off Broadway Shoes. Another good way to get your heels for a cheaper price is to make friends with the sales people in the shoe department at your favorite department store. This way if they like you they may cut you some slack at the register and give you some form of discount. Also, make sure you ask them if there are any current or future promotional sales going on. If not, just wait until the shoe you desire goes on sale and cross your fingers and hope they have the shoe in your size.

JEANS

When buying jeans it may be good to find a pair that flatters you. Whenever you find that jean whether by designer or buy cut, stick with that and run because it will make shopping much easier. There is nothing like a great jean that will make your butt look proportionate with the rest of your body. Ladies make sure when you are trying on jeans you give yourself a thorough look over. This means when you try them on don't just stop at the side view in the jeans, turn around and look at your back view. If you can't see the back view, whip out your foundation mirror and look at that rear view with that. If you see your love handles trying to escape the wrath of those tight jeans, everybody else will see it too. So, I have some information on body types and jeans so you can see what type of jeans flatters your body the most.

PEAR SHAPED: The ideal cut of jeans for you are boot cut because this cut is not too tight and not too relaxed to where it looks like you are wearing your boyfriend's favorite pair of jeans. You also might want to get jeans with a slight flare to help balance out your hips with your shoulders. Stretchy jeans are a good fit for you as well. I know some of you have been eye balling skinny jeans but thought that you could never get away with wearing skinny jeans without drawing all the attention to your thighs. Good news, you can wear skinny jeans, I suggest that you wear them with an A-line top or a top that comes past your hips if you are insecure about them.

SLIM: Many European jeans are longer and fit quite comfortably for this body type. Skinny jeans can give the appearance of a fuller butt or wider hips. You should also consider high waisted wide-leg jeans. Some more good cuts are straight leg, boot cut, high waisted, low waisted, and flared. Just about any jean cut is great since your legs are longer and it doesn't take much to create the illusion of having long legs. Your illusion lies in having curves, so jeans with styled back pockets (True Religion) can give the illusion of having an ample butt.

PETITE: The main idea for you petite ladies is to create an illusion of an extended body and a longer leg. The perfect cuts of jeans are straight leg, skinny, cigarette and wide leg. Make sure when wearing your jeans you check the hem and get the hem tapered if it is too long. You will look even shorter if the bottoms of your jeans are dragging on the ground as you walk. It is also cute to wear heels with boot cut or wide leg jeans because it creates a great couture line and gives a great illusion of longer legs.

Ladies, be open minded with fashion and wear what makes you feel FAB. Don't conform to wearing stilettos to class just because that is what you see other chicks on campus wearing. If you know you are a die hard sneaker fan, keep that look and roll with it. Maybe step your sneaker game up with vintage kicks or sneakers that have color and style. Rock a pair of fitted jeans and some accessories to play up the look of your sneakers. Even though you are a die hard sneaker fan, I know you want to turn a few heads with the male species. Let me repeat, I know YOU want to turn heads with the male species, not your one of a kind vintage kicks! So, you might want to embrace a smidgen of make-up.

MAKE-UP

I know you might not have been a makeup artist while you were in high school, but a dab of foundation and some eye mascara "ain't hurt nobody." But remember to go light on the foundation, cake faces have never been what's up. If you are not seriously into makeup just accent your best facial feature. If your eyes are to die for, you should wear eye mascara and some eye liner or if you have nice lips you should make sure they stay moisturized or glossed. For my more advanced makeup artist, be adventurous and try new colors with your eye shadow. Don't and I repeat don't get too carried away because nobody wants to sit next to the "clown" in class.

HAIR

With having fashion freedom and some money in your pocket; please don't forget about your hair. Some of you, while in high school, never let go of hair gel or child like pony tails; ribbons included....so boo you! This may have been a good look while you were in high school, but while you are in college you might want to let go of some of your bad hair habits. I know some of you feel like you need hair gel like an ashy person needs Vaseline but try something different with your hair. For starters, hair gel (I don't care how clear the gel is) is never a good look for maintaining healthy hair. It dries out and damages your hair just so you can have slick edges. So unless you plan on eventually being edgeless, I advise you to slowly walk away from the hair gel.

You might want to consider going to a hair salon and getting a basic wash and set, this is a healthy style that doesn't require high maintenance. All you have to do is wrap your hair at night and unwrap it in the morning before you go to class. On a side note, wrap your hair with a silk scarf because those cotton bandanas are a no-go. A wash and set can have your hair flowing in the wind no matter how short or thick your hair is. I know you are thinking that you can't go to a hair salon every week, but if you can I suggest that you go once a month or twice a month. In between time, you can wash your own hair and if you are not getting that salon look at home, ask your hair stylist what products they are using on your hair. You should buy those products and get to work on your hair.

For those of you that are not satisfied with the length of your hair try adding that desired length with hair extensions. You may be surprised at how many chicks you see on campus with long flowing hair that are probably rocking some silky straight hair extensions. Hair extensions are a great look as long as your tracks are hidden. For those of you that have never worn hair extensions, please remember that your real hair is somewhere beneath all of those hair extensions. Trust me; you may go bald if you don't attend to your real hair underneath the hair extensions. So, don't forget to wash your hair weekly or bi-weekly when you have extensions.

I recommend that you get a sew-in or a quick weave (tracks are glued to a stocking cap and weave is worn as a wig) and please refrain from frequent use of hair glue applied to your scalp. When getting a quick weave do not allow someone to place a stocking cap on your head and start the gluing process. You should wear a plastic cap under the stocking cap to avoid hair glue from being applied to your hair. If you decide to get a glue-in, I would assume that it would be pretty hard to wash your hair every week with hair glue applied to your scalp. So make sure extensions applied with glue are not kept in long.

*L*adies, have fun with your new sense of fashion and make sure you feel great when you step outside of your dorm. Be creative and wear what makes you feel fabulous when you see your reflection in the mirror. Always remember to take care of the hair on your head so that your hair doesn't decide to leave you because you decided to perm it and color it all in the same month. You gets no love from your hair which will result in the strands of you hair giving up; thus beginning the process of you balding.

EMBRACING ADULTHOOD

When you graduate from high school and start to embark on college, you might not notice much of a physical change with yourself. When you get to college you will probably look pretty much the same as when you left high school....that acne might clear up but that might be the only physical change you notice. Even though you probably won't notice a physical change you will definitely notice a mental change during your first semester of college when you realize your parents aren't there to wake you up for school. I will go through some of the changes that you may face as you are embracing adulthood in college.

ENDLESS FREEDOM

Your world will open up to an unfamiliar level of freedom since your parents probably controlled your every move while in school. You will no longer need your parent's permission to go out at night, so the "Let me ask my parents" training wheels will officially be removed when your college experience begins.

One major change in your life will be the ultimate freedom you have while in college. Nobody is there to force you to go to class; it's pretty much your decision. Regardless of if you go or not your tuition is paying for that class session, so honestly; some professors could care less if you showed your face in their class because they will get paid even if you don't show up. You will need to use common sense and stay focused on the main objective in college…which is to graduate. With this ultimate freedom there will come more responsibility and adult decisions to be made because you might not be living in the same PG-rated living environment you lived in while growing up. Your parents might have attempted to shield you from a lot of the dangers in the world while you were living under their roof. Well, be prepared because a lot of what they were protecting you from may be waiting for you when you get to college.

<u>ARE THOSE DRUGS?</u>

A lot of colleges are known for their amazing academic programs, but they may be unaware of their advanced underground alcohol and drugs programs being offered to undergraduates. Clearly you didn't read about any of this on their college brochure. You might be in a situation where your new college friends are smoking marijuana and someone decides to pass you the joint, even though you expressed to your friends that you do not have weed head aspirations. At this moment you will be faced with an adult decision, do you take a toke (take a puff) but don't inhale the marijuana into your lungs so you can fit in and not get high (good luck with that whole not getting high thing), or do you stand your ground and tell your friends that you aren't an occasional weed smoker. Whatever your decision would be in a situation like this (I'm crossing my fingers you take the second option), it will be an adult decision.

What you non-druggies may not know is that drugs like marijuana can lead you to other drugs like ecstasy, cocaine, heroine and methamphetamines. Once you get used to the high of smoking marijuana, a friend of yours might introduce you to another drug (cocaine) that might get you even higher than marijuana, hence the beginning of the downward spiral of your life.

PARTIES AND CLASSES

Another adult decision will be what you decide to do during your spare time. Most colleges don't have a curfew for you to be in your dorm, which means that you can come and go as you please. It will be your decision whether or not you go out to a party the night before a big exam and come back to your dorm at 3:00 a.m. Don't think that all the hottest parties are only held on Friday and Saturday nights, that's rarely the case. A lot of parties are held during the week, depending on what school you attend and how the party scene is on campus, around campus, and in the city nearest to your campus.

When I was in college, I would finish any papers I had due or projects that needed to be turned in before I even considered going to any party. Please let it be known that I got ahead academically by doing this, because partying was my hobby of choice while I was in college. Basically, you will have to learn how to balance both partying and your academics, which will make you more responsible at the end of the day. However, I don't recommend partying the night before a big exam. People that party before a big exam already know they are going to fail the exam; but this won't be your situation because you have real dreams of one day graduating from college.

INDIVIDUALITY

With all of this freedom you may find time to discover your new sense of individuality. While growing up you probably didn't get to express yourself as you wanted because your parents held a dictatorship in their house. You might have spent countless hours fantasizing of the day you could cut your hair off, grow dreads, and let them run free in the wind. Once you go to college you can cut your hair off and start growing those dreads you've dreamed of.

While in college you might notice the things that make you a unique individual and you will come to find that you do have a voice and you can stand up for what you want. Since your parents can't really control what you do with your body, you get to decide what you want to do with it. Once you're over the age of eighteen, you don't need your parent's signature to get things like a tattoo or a piercing. It is solely up to you what you want written across your lower back for the rest of your life....so think wisely or get a temporary tattoo, maybe Henna, until you are ready for the real thing.

With many of the decisions you make you might want to think, "What would my parents say if they could see me right now?" If that makes you think twice about guzzling down beer from a hose attached to a funnel then, by all means, keep this thought in your head at all times. I'm pretty sure even though some of you will think this, you will still be the one drinking from that hose while all the people in the room yell, "Chug, Chug, Chug!" At the end of the day you are an adult now and you will decide what you are comfortable doing in your free time. Just keep in mind that your adult-like decisions will come with adult-like consequences.

Gentle reminders…

- Every action comes with a reaction of some sort; so partying all the time and neglecting your academics will result in you being put on academic probation.
- "Say No to Drugs," taking prescription medicine not prescribed to you for non-medical reasons is considered a drug, as well as the other well known illegal drugs.
- At the very moment your parents are waving goodbye to you as they leave your campus, you will become an adult; let's make that a responsible adult.
- When planning your social outings, factor in your academics so that you get more accomplished academically than socially.
- Take this time of freedom and being an adult to become your own individual.
- Always remember that you are in college to one day graduate and do not let anything defer you from that purpose.

RULES: DATING, PARTYING, AND DORM ROOM VISITS

*N*ow keep in mind that you may be dating guys that have not reached their full level of maturity and quite frankly some probably never will, which sucks. Therefore you have to know what you are willing to deal with and never settle for less. If there is one thing to keep in mind when dating; never settle for less than what you deserve in a mate. Whatever he does that gets on your nerves now will probably still get on your nerves five years from now. For some of you, this may be your first time dating or even being alone with a guy without your parents breathing over your shoulder. That's why you must recognize game when you see it and keep it moving if the guy you like isn't treating you right nor respecting you.

I'm telling you this because I know you would much rather spend your time doing something you enjoy rather than crying over some guy. I have some rules that I follow personally and if you like my dating rules you should use them too.

1. **Never kiss on the first date**.

   Reason: I know his lips may look delectable and soft, but please refrain from giving him a kiss…that is unless he saves your life during dinner by performing the Heimlich maneuver because you were choking on some food then, by all means, grab some lip palm and pucker up. Seriously, kissing a guy passionately on the first date (especially if you really like him) might make you try to rush things emotionally and make it hard to enjoy the friendly stage of courting.

What to do: If you find yourself at the awkward moment when you are saying your farewells with your date and he is gazing in your eyes and he slowly leans in for a kiss, you should slowly lean in for a hug. As you are leaning in, turn your head slightly at a 45 degree angle so that his kiss lands on your cheek and then wish him a safe trip home.

2. **Text or call him once and leave a message.**

    Reason: Communication is imperative in any relationship and there is no communication if you are the only one communicating. If he doesn't return your phone calls or text you back, he probably isn't thinking about you and doesn't understand common courtesy.

    What to do: When calling someone make sure you leave a voicemail because dudes love to say that they never received a call or a text message; but it's hard to tell a fib and say that you didn't receive a voicemail.

3. **Never seem too available.**

    Reason: This lets him get too comfortable with the thought that he can see you whenever he wants to. You shouldn't let a dude interrupt your quality time of hanging out with your girls or your quality time with yourself. Basically, do not jump at his every request to see you and drop what you are doing or cancel previous plans that you may have made.

    What to do: When he calls and wants to get up with you, politely let him know that you already have plans and that maybe the two or you can get up another time. Please do not see this rule as "playing games," however; see this as having your own space and not letting yourself get to the point where you will ditch your friends or previous plans at the drop of a dime because some dude wants to spend time with you.

4. **Do not make it a habit of hanging out in his bedroom**.

   Reason: The television, restroom, computer, and everything else in the living room work just fine; the only thing that doesn't work in the living room is a bed. When you sit and get too comfortable in a guys bed it can easily lead to you lying down on his bed to get a little bit more comfortable and this can lead to you being under the covers in a sticky situation.

   What to do: Make it a habit of either not hanging out at his place or not hanging out in his bedroom.

5. **Never do the "At Home Movie Night" for the first date**.

   Reason: Refer to the chapter, *To Date or Not to Date*

   What to do: Watch a movie at the movie theater for the first date.

6. **Conduct yourself like a lady on a date**.

   Reason: Always know that whatever you do a third party will know. I know you are going to tell your BFF and he is going to tell his, so there, the cat is already out the bag.

   What to do: Be mindful of this and refrain from acting like you do not have any home training.

7. **Try not to ride in cars with strangers**.

   Reason: Just because you and this wonderful guy talked on the phone last night for three hours straight does not mean he is no longer a stranger. You wouldn't be able to pick up on his violent tendencies during that three hour conversation.

What to do: Make it a point to meet at the dating location, if you don't have transportation invite one of your friends with a car and make it a double date.

8. **No dating after 10:00 p.m.**

   Reason: Nothing good can come of going on a date after 10:00 p.m. What can the two of you possibly do after 10:00 p.m. that won't lead you back to his place? Done thinking, was your list of activities long? I doubt it....on to the next rule.

   What to do: If a guy invites you out after 10:00 p.m. decline the offer and let him know that you will be available to spend time with him during the day. If you just feel like you have to get out of your dorm that late, go somewhere with your girls.

9. **Always tell someone who you are going on a date with and where.**

   Reason: This is safe just in case you end up in a bad situation while on a date, at least people will know where you were going and information about your date.

   What to do: Tell someone where you are even if you tell your best friend that lives in another state. Make sure you tell your friend his name, number, a brief description of him, and his license plate number if possible.

10. **Chivalry is not dead...you just might have to re-introduce it to guys.**

    Reason: I feel as though there are some things dudes are just supposed to do like open the door for a female or when walking on a sidewalk a dude should walk nearest the street. Things like this are chivalrous and shows you that he treats you like a queen.

    What to do: If you meet a dude and he is not chivalrous, introduce him to it. When walking up to a door, step aside so that he can open the door for you. Give him the opportunity to be chivalrous where you see fit, if he doesn't get the hint, leave him for a dude that has some real home training.

11. **Never assume a dude is going to pay**

    Reason: My friend invited me to go to a lounge with her and her doctor friend and she said that everything would be taken care of. Let's just say that by the end of the night he got up and took out a $20 (for his drink) and laid it ever so politely on the table and left us with the tab....I might as well had thrown away $45.00 that night.

    What to do: Always keep money on you just in case he does not intend on paying or is short on funds and can not cover the whole tab. Don't forget this experience and remember it in case he asks you out again.

12. **Never settle for the title, "Friends with Benefits"**

    Reason: An exclusive friend with benefits is a no win situation. There is an old saying, "Why buy the cow when you can get the milk for free." If you are playing the role of girlfriend without the commitment, why would he want to make a commitment with you?

    What to do: Make sure the two of you have a clear understanding on whether or not the two of you are in a monogamous relationship. If the two of you are not in a relationship don't act like it, and continue be "just friends."

13. **If he says, "I am not looking for a relationship"…he means it.**

    Reason: When a guy says that he doesn't want a girlfriend that is basically what he means, so do not fall into the trap of playing the role of his girlfriend because seven months later he will most likely still not want to be in a relationship. Those seven months will be nothing but wasted energy put into a "relationship" that was non-existent before it had a chance to be.

What to do: Treat him like a friend and be his friend…nothing more and nothing less. Do not cross the girlfriend line and think that if you play the role of his girlfriend that eventually he will change his mind and decide that he wants to be in a relationship with you. I doubt he will change his mind and when you tell him that you are tired of him not being able to commit to a relationship he will probably let you know that he told you in the beginning that he wasn't looking for a girlfriend. Which will leave you stuck looking confused with a broken heart.

PARTYING

There will come a time where you are out and about and you just happen to bump into a handsome guy that you can envision being your future suitor, or husband….if you think that far ahead at first glance. This guy can be a complete stranger or a guy that you have a slight crush on; don't act like you haven't doodled his name when you were bored in class. You must know how to keep your cool and act like him and all that is fine is not that big of a deal to you. You meet dudes like this all the time right? I have some pointers on how to seem interested in him when you see him, but not so interested to where you seem creepy and slightly stalker-like.

- When you see this dude at a party do not make a mad dash to speak to him first. If the two of you happen to cross paths, speak to him, but don't seem too anxious to see his dreamy smile.

- If you are at a party and you happen to speak to a guy that you like, make small talk and go about your business. I wouldn't recommend that you stay in his vicinity too long because you will seem too pressed to be in his company. You came to the event to hang out with your chicas, not hang out with his shadow.

- When you are at a party and you see your crush, observe him. The way he handles himself in a social atmosphere says a lot about him. If you see him grinding up on every chick at the event, would you still be crushing him? I know that he is not your boyfriend and is not in any type of committed relationship, but why make that wild beast into your future boo?

- Let's say that you are at a party and the guy that you have been eye-balling all night has just tapped you on the shoulder to talk to you. I know you might be super excited that you are engaging in conversation with this dude, but keep it short. After a couple of minutes of talking tell him, "It was nice meeting you or it was nice to see you (depends on it you know him or not), but I am about to go with my girls." If he is digging you he will make it a point to snag your number before you walk away or at least before you leave the party.

- Do not dance with every dude at a party; and don't dance so wild to where it looks like you are conceiving a child. I can not stress this to you enough; this is never a good look. On top of it making you look like a wild child, you will sweat out your hair in the process and I know you did not spend twenty minutes curling your hair for nothing.

- If you are at a house party, take note of where the nearest exits are...just in case the cops come, trust me; they usually come. Not that cops are bad or anything, they just weren't invited to the house party and people tend to bust a sprint when cops do come. To avoid getting trampled, I suggest you post up by the door at a house party.

- Do not give out your phone number to every dude that looks your way at a party. If you know that you don't want to get to know him further than now, why give him your phone number? At the end of the day he wants to be more than friends so why waste your energy dodging his phone calls?

- On a side note, ladies; do not wear shades at night to a club or to a party....save that foolishness for the dudes. This is just my personal pet peeve and it doesn't make a lick of sense. Trust me; you will not look exclusive, mysterious, or anything that you think you might look like with shades on at night.

DORM ROOM VISITS

The one big thing I know some of you can't wait on is being around a guy without your parents in the next room. Some of you have never had a boy sit on your bed, let alone be in a room alone with him... with the door closed and locked. Since this is going to be new to you, there might be some things to consider when having these dorm room visits.

- For starters, don't let a dude stay in your room past a certain time that you set yourself. I mean seriously, what can a dude possibly say to you at 3:00 a.m. besides, "I got a condom." There is something about a full moon and having your not-so-attractive homeboy in your dorm room at night, if that moonlight hits him at the right angle; he might start to look super cute.

- When hanging out with a guy in his dorm room, try not to sit on his bed. Well, if you do sit on his bed, don't get too comfortable; too comfortable to the point where the two of you are laid up because that can lead to other things. Just make sure you don't lie down at any point during your visit because that twin bed is a trap.
- Do not over-extend your stay in his dorm room; it's a dorm room visit, not an extended stay motel.
- If you live in apartment style housing, do not let your boyfriend turn his visits into a permanent live-in situation. I don't care how much of an apartment aura your dorm has, it is still a dorm.

I know that you may not follow all of these rules but I know I wish I would have had someone give me some guidelines on how to date when I was a freshman in college. I knew nothing and my friends and I were up a creek without a paddle when it came to dating guys. We kind of just learned from each other's mistakes when it came down to guys. I hope these rules are helpful with your newfound navigation in the dating world.

TO DATE OR NOT TO DATE

ollege guys are basically broke guys with potential. They are ambitious, goal driven and, even though you might not see it yet, they will someday be potential husband material to someone. One drawback with dating a college guy may be finances; you can only go walking through the park for free so many times before it gets old. Even though that guy in your science class is cute, the guy that drove by in that Range Rover on your way to that science class is even cuter. With this being said, your dating realm may broaden while in college and you may choose to date guys that are not necessarily enrolled in college with you.

Dating in college may be more complicated than dating in high school since your parents may not be there to dictate your relationships anymore. While in college I doubt you will need to sneak and kiss your boyfriend before your third period class nor will you have to orchestrate a way to meet your boyfriend at the movies. Once your parents leave you on campus you are pretty much thrown into the adult world of dating; if you choose to date at all. Since you will probably be new to this, I will help give you some pointers on how to navigate through the dating scene and provide you with some information on the types of guys you may encounter.

NO CURFEWS

For many of you curfews will be a thing of the past, except for when you go home on the holidays because you know your parents are not about to let you embark on any late night adventures while you are sleeping under their roof. At first, you might find joy in coming back to your dorm at 3:00 a.m.; hey, you've never seen what the moon looks like around that time. Just because you can be out until the wee hours of the morning with some dude doesn't mean that you should.

In regards to dating, I don't recommend you entertaining potential suitors late at night. If a guy can not find time to spend with you during the day; that poses a problem. There are 24 hours in a day and the last three hours of a day should not be devoted to you. Just be smart and recognize if a dude only wants to see you at night, even though you will have the ability to drive to his house at 11:00 p.m. doesn't make it right. Dates do not start after 10:00 p.m. at his house, those aren't dates; let's keep it real we all know what that's all about. He might claim that all he wants to do is cuddle, but know that the word cuddle is nothing more than a gentle word for sex. So, unless you are prepared to fight off those octopus arms, tell him that you are busy tonight and he can catch you tomorrow…during the day.

AT HOME MOVIE NIGHT

When I was in college, guys would recommend that we watch a movie at their place for the first date, but unbeknownst to them I already knew what was up…I was already forewarned about this type of date. We will just call this the "At Home Movie Night" date. This is so not a first date; it is nothing but a set-up for your new boo to try his luck at getting intimate with you. He may tell you that his intentions are not to have sex with you; but I'm pretty darn sure that he hopes that the night ends that way.

I am about to play out the whole "At Home Movie Night" date for you. First, you go over to his place around 7:00 p.m. and of course you are not going to start watching the movie once you get there. You guys will engage in small talk and eventually he will push play on his DVD player. After the movie is over, it may be 10:00 p.m. and by now you are comfortable being over there. Your heels are off and the two of you have managed to get real cozy and couple-like on the couch. By now he has told you how down to earth you are, how he thinks you're pretty enough to be a model and how fine you look in those tight jeans. If he is old school, or has an older brother, he will either mention to you that he gives an amazing back rub or somehow try to bet you that he can give you the best back rub you've ever had.

If he is about his game he will have real massage oil but if you are dating that broke college guy I mentioned earlier, he may have lotion. Please take note as to how empty that massage oil is, because if it looks like he would be dabbing the last couple of drops on you; know that he has given quite a few massages before you came along. Whatever the case may be do not go for the back rub. The sensation from his hands rubbing your back may cause an increase in your hormone level and the next thing you know you are laid out half dressed in his bed telling him, "I don't usually do this." I know you may be laughing but guys really do this and once the bra pops off, it's a wrap. So ladies, do not fall for the back rub…you have been warned.

THE OLD MAN

You are about to begin a chapter in your life where you may be the target age for older men. When I say older men, I mean men that are in

71

their thirties or older; that's older when you are all of eighteen years old. These men may seem enticing because they are past that broke college stage and are in career mode; they tend to be more financially well off than the typical college guy. So ladies, this is the time where you set an age limit for dating. Please believe a lot of older men do not set an age limit for dating, even if you are the same age as their oldest child. For those of you that are intrigued with the thought of dating one of these old men there are some things you need to know.

Some of these men are married, and if he tells you that he and his wife are "separated," he is still legally married so keep it moving. Never assume the relationship status of an older man when he approaches you for your phone number. Some married men find no shame in asking for a pretty ladies phone number, so make it a point to ask whether he is married or not. He might be married if he never, and I mean never, invites you over to his house or he never calls you at night. He does not do these things because he is at home playing the role of husband and father. His wife is probably crazy and his kids probably know karate, so unless you want some deranged wife and her nun-chucking kids coming after you; I suggest you leave the married type alone. Before you decide to get serious with an old man, think about how your wedding will look with your young vibrant bridesmaids and his old geriatric groomsmen… it's just a thought.

THE RAPPER/PRODUCER

Depending on where your college is located you may notice that every guy you meet is a rapper or a producer…or they pretty much have those aspirations. Ask him what pays the bills and let it be known that whatever pays the bills is his real job. So if he tells you that he is a rapper but he works at a department store by day then, by golly, at the end of the day he is a cashier at a department store. I am not trying to crush anybodies dreams but you have to be real about the situation and a dude shouldn't feel the need to lie to you about what pays the bills. He should say, "I work at a department store and my dream is to become a rapper because music runs through my blood," and so forth and so on. Now once rapping starts paying the bills then rapping will be his source of income, hence his job.

Ladies, do not make frequent trips to the recording studio with a dude, especially if he is not your boyfriend. There is no point of you being there and quite frankly it may make you look like a groupie. Does he really need you in the recording studio for moral support so he can spit five bars? Now, unless you have future music industry aspirations I advise you to pass on the trips to the recording studio. This is just my opinion, I know there are going to be some of you sitting in the studio for four hours straight while your future rapper boo drops a couple of verses, because he is rapping about you right.....yeah about that.

Dear Keesh,

There is this guy that I have been seeing for a while, he has the swagger that I go for and he is financially well off. The only problem is I don't really know how he earns his income. I am almost certain that his income is illegally funded but I love the gifts and the finer things that he is able to give me. What should I do?

Sincerely,
-Hugs for Thugs

I recommend that you remove yourself from this relationship immediately. No man is worth loosing your future over. Please believe if the feds catch up with your dude you may be serving as much time as he is in jail; depending on how illegal his operations are. Go ahead and be a ride-or-die chick for your dude and see how far that gets you. I'm going to tell you, it isn't going to get you far at all; it is just going to give you a free pass to jail with a butch chick saying, "what's up new bootie." There should be no amount of money or gifts that will have you second guessing whether or not you want to enjoy your future as a free woman. I'm going to need you to ask him what he really does for a living and if he says something that sounds the least bit illegal, (in the words of my Maury Povich fans) "Drop that zero for a hero!"

-Keesh

THE CLEAN DIRTIES

While I was in college there was "the strip," it was a road that ran through campus and it was notorious for being a spot to hang out. Some colleges have an area like this, ladies' be aware of this hang out spot. At night the strip would become a car show of sorts because men would ride through (with no educational purpose) and pick up college chicks. At first, this can be very appealing because you are meeting a guy with an $80,000 Mercedes Benz and you think that he is very successful and has his life together. Just know that everything that glitters isn't gold.

You can not look at a dude and think that you know what he is about because there are guys that "lease" for the image of success. This means that he does not own the things that you look at while you are thinking about how successful he is. That Mercedes Benz he is pushing is being leased; not because he likes getting new cars every other year but because he really can not afford to own the car. The condo on the twenty-third floor with the amazing view of the downtown city lights is his cousin's (who is away because he plays in the league) but you would never know because he kicks it to you like it is his. This is a dirty dude with clean clothes on because he is creating an illusion of a lifestyle he doesn't own. So, be mindful that you should not judge a guy by the car he drives or the life he claims to live because he may not be what he appears to be.

THE HIGHSCHOOL SWEET TART

Your high school sweetheart may be the first guy you fell in love with and he is the only guy that has the key to your heart. I'm going to keep it real and let you know that high school relationships may be hard to bring into your new college life. Between meeting new people (dudes) and the distance between you and your sweet tart, things can get difficult within the relationship. If you know that he is the guy that you are destined to marry then, by all means, stay with him. But if you are on the fence about the relationship let it go and just remain friends. This is a time for the two of you to grow, explore, and experience life.

I don't want you ladies to think that I am making this entire high school sweetheart thing up, so I took the liberty of interviewing some females about their college relationships. The answers varied a lot so for those of you that intend on marrying your high school sweetheart there is still hope.

1. *Did your high school relationship carry into college?*

Majority of the females interviewed stated that they did have a boyfriend prior to college. Their boyfriends were a source of comfort as they started their college experience. They knew that they could call their dudes when they had a rough day in class and needed to vent. So, for you engaged and underage types there may be a sense of comfort in knowing that you have a secure relationship already and you might be more willing to patch things up when your future hubby steps out of line. Other chicks that had a boyfriend pretty much forgot about them when they got to college because they were meeting so many new people. They would forget to do the little things like call their boyfriends back or fail to fall through with plans to spend time together.

On the other hand, the girls that came into college single felt a since of freedom because they were not in a relationship. Since they did not have a boyfriend they were not obligated to make time for anyone but themselves. Many of them were happy that they did not have to deal with the ups and downs of a relationship on top of getting used to college life. Regardless of if you decide to come into college with your high school sweet tart, you may want to consider if the relationship will be a hassle or a great experience for you two to enjoy.

2. Was it hard to maintain your relationship while you were in college?

Some girls felt like it wasn't that hard to maintain their relationship because they went to a college in a different state from their boyfriends. The fact that they did not see each other often made the relationship really simple. Not all the girls felt this way though, some felt as though going to school in a different state than their high school boos was difficult. In high school, you may have seen your high school sweet pea everyday by your locker after third period and the lack of seeing each other once the two of you leave for college may create a problem.

Others that attended college in the same city as their high school sweetie realized that their newfound freedom was harder to manage between college friends and their boyfriend, since there were times when they had to choose between the two. One girl mentioned that while she was a freshman in college she continued dating her high school sweetie and it was hard for her because he was always around her. At one point she was torn between going somewhere to hang out with him and going to the homecoming concert; let me tell you, she said that homecoming concert was dope. She knew that she wanted to enjoy her college experience so after the concert her and her boyfriend had a long conversation about her choosing to go to the concert versus spending time together. After everything was said and done they came to an understanding and he realized that he had to give her some space. Regardless of if you and your boyfriend are in the same state or thousands of miles apart you will have to make time for each other to make the relationship work. If you are willing to make it work, buckle up and get ready for the ride.

3. *How often did you see each other while you were in college?*

For the girls that attended college in a separate state than their boyfriends, they didn't get to see their high school sweeties that often. These ladies mostly saw them during holidays, the summer, and whenever they went back home to visit. The ladies that lived in the same state as their boyfriends saw them more often. This posed a problem for some because they did not feel as though they were enjoying college life due to their boyfriends' constant demands to be around.

It may be easier to maintain a long distance relationship because at the end of the day, the two of you are nothing more than lovers via the internet, web cam, video mail, or cell phone…don't forget, those minutes aren't free until after seven! On a side note; do not, and I repeat, do not base your college of choice off your boyfriend. Just because your boyfriend received a full scholarship doesn't mean you need to enjoy it with him at the same college. You are going to be mad as crap when the two of you break-up and now you are enrolled in a college in no-mans-land, Oregon.

4. *Did you spend a lot of time crying over your boyfriend?*

Some of the stories that were mentioned on why tears were shed are practical because relationships come with ups and downs. Some girls didn't expect their relationships to end so abruptly because they thought that their relationships were stable prior to college. They didn't know how to handle being away from their boyfriends and it just became difficult to maintain no matter how hard they tried to keep things together. With any real relationship there are going to be hard times so you have to know if you are strong enough to handle crying over your dude all night and then wake up in the morning to take your biology exam. So you can save yourself the headache, tissue, and drama if you walk onto your college campus single…just thought I would slide that it.

Ladies know this, you might not realize it right now, but there is a world out there that you have yet to embark on. Take a second and think about your life ten years from now; are you sure that you want to be gazing into your high school sweetheart's crusty eyes? Ladies know that there is no guy worth the tears or the drama especially when you are young, marvelous, and fierce!

5. Did you cheat on your boyfriend while you were in college?

This response varied because high school relationships are different from college relationships. One major difference is the absence of parental control because your parents are no longer the ones dictating your relationships with guys; so basically; your dating training wheels are taken off when you get to college. The ladies that were seriously in love with their boyfriends did not betray them and remained faithful. Some girls stated that they cheated on their boyfriends a couple of months into college while other girls did not cheat but their boyfriends had wondering tendencies. Ladies, if your lab partner's lips start looking too tempting, I advise you to either switch lab partners or chuck your high school sweetie those deuces.

6. How long did your high school relationship last while you were in college?

This answer varied in response but there was one common statement made, "we broke up." Whether it was an "I don't want to see your face ever again," type of break-up or an "I just need some space," kind of break-up where you are back together within weeks. Majority of the females at some point in time took a break from their relationships.

One girl that was still with her boyfriend from high school at the time being interviewed stated that her and her high school sweetie broke up numerous of times while in college. She knew that they both loved each other dearly and every time they would break up, a couple of days later her and her turtle dove would get back together.

This may or may not be your situation if you are bringing your high school sweetie on for the ride in college. Majority of the chicks that were interviewed stated that their relationships ended during their freshmen year. You must know for yourself when it is time to let go, once again let me reiterate that you are young and oh so fabulous and there is time for you to get super serious about a guy…like when your 30!

7. Did you have anymore relationships' while in college?

Some of the ladies, who seemed like serial daters, got into other relationships while in school. Some ladies dated guys at other colleges, and some dated guys that went to their school. The relationships were not always with a college guy though. Some ladies dated older guys that were not in school, this is where you determine what kind of guy you are truly interested in. I personally didn't seriously date another guy while I was in college. I was too busy having fun to argue, cry, and settle down with a guy. I was too busy discovering myself; I didn't have time to discover somebody else.

8. Would you recommend carrying over high school relationships into college?

Many responses depended on how strong the relationship was entering into college. If the relationship was shaky in high school it is not worth bringing into college; why add more stress to the college experience? Basically, you should factor in the type of dude you are dealing with; if he cheated on you in high school, I doubt that his cheating ways are going to cease and desist in college. You should also consider the potential longevity of your relationship because if you are borderline tired of him while you are in high school, let that relationship go because you will be bored with him in college. On the flip side, some ladies stated that bringing their relationships to college was a great experience for them and their boyfriends were a great support system when adjusting to college. So, if you and your high school sweetie have a bright future then stick along for the journey and see if your relationship works out while you are in college.

9. Are you and your high school sweet tart still friends?

Great news, a lot of females mentioned that they have managed to maintain a friendship with their high school sweetie. So, if your relationship hits the dumps you can still be friends. Of course, after the two of you get over the fact that hearts were broken in the relationship, you can build a friendship. There were a few chicks that stated that they could not really be friends with their ex-boos. When asked if they would speak to their ex-boos if they crossed paths walking down the street, they said they would speak which is a great sign; hey, being associates still counts. Ha! You might not be homies but you can still be great friends that talk on social networking sites from time to time.

Dear Keesh,

My boyfriend and I broke up not too long ago, and now I am going home for the holidays and I know I am going to be tempted to rekindle that flame. He told me that he loves me and that he has changed and wants to work things out. I don't think that I can leave him alone or let him out of my life because I feel like at the end of the day, he is the one for me. Should I give him another chance at a relationship?

Sincerely,
-Ex Lover Sob Story

This is a difficult situation for you to be in. On one hand you probably love this guy and dream of getting married and having five kids with him. On the other hand you know that the two of you had a rough time managing a relationship; hence the reason why the two of you are no longer in a relationship. One thing I can say to you is that you will never be able to move on if you never let go of what you had. Until you decide for yourself what's the healthiest relationship for you and your ex-boo, you will constantly be back and forth with him and you won't give other great guys the chance to get to know you. Wake up and decide what is right for you and stick with your decision. The fact that you feel like you can not leave him alone is nothing but hogwash! You should never feel like you can not let a dude go, trust me; you will not stop breathing if he stops calling you.

-Keesh

I am going to let you know that your relationship in college may not be as magical as those in the movies. Your new boy toy may not be your Prince Charming, and quite frankly, he just might be a jerk. You have to know what you are willing to deal with because if he starts off as a jerk chances are he is going to continue to be a jerk. Ladies your first year in school is a time for you to be young, remarkable, and liberated while you are adjusting to college life.

This is the time for you to form new friendships, hang out with new friends, and create lasting memories. You can use this time to focus on yourself and better yourself. There is time for you to get serious with a guy and if you feel like that time is now, go for it; but if not, have fun marching to the beat of your own drum. If you do decide to get into a relationship it should make you feel happy and not stressed out. You're dating; you're not married so save all that stress for when you are married with five kids and have a mortgage.

Keep in mind...

- When dating, if you feel as though the relationship is not working you should speak up and chuck those deuces, never ignore your intuition.
- If you meet a guy and he claims to be a modern day renaissance man and he owns all of these companies and so forth…Google him to find out what he says is true.
- Rule of thumb; never date a man that is married, engaged, separated, or currently in a relationship. On top of this being flat out trifling, it is bad karma.
- Never settle; if you are not into guys that have dirty nails, gold teeth, and wears more jewelry than you and you happen to meet this guy…keep it moving.

- Communication is imperative in any relationship and if there is no equal communication, there is no relationship.

- Even if you are in a relationship, make time to "do you" and spend time away from your boyfriend.

- If your relationship ends due to your boyfriend breaking up with you, do not make this an opportunity to second guess yourself as if you are not a wonderful person. All relationships are not destined to last forever, and that was one of them.

- After a break-up make a list of the things you didn't like about your ex-boyfriend (ex: snores, not romantic, doesn't listen), read it and know that now that is another chick's problem.

- Whenever you leave a relationship, learn from it so that you don't make the same mistakes when choosing your next boyfriend.

- Ladies, never try to change a guy because it is waste of time and effort. If he doesn't call you enough or make enough of an effort to spend time together, you should leave. You don't want to start a situation where you feel like you are dating yourself and you are the one making all the plans and putting forth all the effort while he never upholds his end of the relationship. You should not have to teach a guy how you deserve to be treated; that my dear, should be natural instinct.

- When dating, the female-to-male ratio may look grim for you; if you want to date a guy from your college. Be mindful that guys on college campuses do communicate with each other. So, be careful when choosing the guy you are crushing because you never know what two guys will become best buds. The last thing you want is your old crush (that you made out with) and your new crush (that you made out with) hanging out together in front of the cafeteria and you walk by...that's awkward.

- I suggest that you broaden you're dating horizon and consider dating outside of your race if a guy of a different race walks by and you can't tear your eyes off him. I know some of you would factor in whether or not your friends or family would approve of this possible relationship. Well, at the end of the day you're a grown woman and you shouldn't feel like there is a stigma against inter-racial dating; you will be opening up yourself to a new experience.

ATHLETES & GREEKS

*D*epending on what college you attend, one or both or these groups of guys are going to be in high demand on the dating scene because they are typically the focal points on campus. Being high in demand translates to stiff competition from other females that want the title of "girlfriend." Some chicks see these guys as a future financial investment because they think that these guys are going to have a lucrative career.

Since some of these relationships are formed with financial hopes in the future, these chicks want to get paid at the end of the day and not work hard for it (well at least not work hard with a real JOB). Ladies, there is a new breed of chicks out there and it might have been easy to date the quarterback in high school, but it might pose a challenge in college. Trust me when I say these chicks will do darn near anything to get into a relationship with an athlete or a Greek on campus. After they get into this relationship, they will probably stop at nothing to keep that relationship. I know some of you are wondering what is in the mind's of these guys...well I interviewed some of them so you won't play yourself when you meet them and you will already know what's up. Here we go:

1. *What were the chances of you holding a real relationship during your freshman year?*

For the most part, majority of the guys interviewed stated that their chances were slim to none of holding a real relationship; unless they came to school with a girlfriend. Some of the guys came into college in a relationship with their high school sweetie's but the relationships ended during their freshmen year due to the distance, adjustments to college life, and the arguments that occurred. Some guys stated that they worked hard to make things work with their girlfriends during their freshmen year. A couple dudes mentioned that they felt like a kid in the candy store when it came to college chicks because a lot of girls were trying to get at them and now they had the freedom to really holla back. Relationships can be harder to manage in college and some guys didn't want to go through the stress of maintaining a serious relationship.

2. *What words do you and your boys use to describe a "groupie?"*

A lot of the guys just used the term groupie but there were other terms used as well. A "bopper" is a chick that bounces from dude to dude and from sport to sport. This kind of chick may be the running back's special fan during the football season and the point guard's special fan during basketball season. She can't make up her mind on who she wants to date so she dates them all in hopes of making an athlete into a boyfriend. Other terms like "kleat chaser," "bust down," and "jump-off" were also used. None of these words sound flattering and you don't want to be known as: "(your name here) the jump-off!" So be mindful of your actions because college is like high school in the spirit of gossiping.

3. *How do you know when a girl tries too hard to get at you?*

Most of the responses dealt with girls that call too much, always want to be around, and pretty much throws themselves at them. See, I didn't tell you ladies to call once and seem busy for nothing. Some of you may feel like calling your crush lets him know that you are thinking about him, but let him know that you have other, more important things on your mind…that do not involve him. Guys notice when a girl is trying too hard to get their attention and don't seem to have a life of their own. One guy mentioned that he knew when a chick was trying too hard when she was constantly around him and his fraternity brothers. It's like she had no reason to be around but she was just there chatting it up like she was in the fraternity.

A common response was that girls do whatever these guys want them to do before they even get to know them. Take a note from *Coming to America* when Prince Akeem rejects his future bride because she doesn't have a mind of her own and was willing to give into his every demand. If a guy asks you for something simple like a piece of gum, cool; if you have it give him a piece if you like. But if this same guy asks you for fifty dollars to get a boot off his car, tell him that won't be possible but he can use your cell phone to call another chick that is dumb enough to give him the money.

One guy said that a girl approached him at the club and seemed to know more about him than he did. Ladies, I know you might have searched for information of the star athlete of your school on the internet but please don't act like you know him personally; especially if the two of you haven't formally met. So, don't say, "Hey, you're Troy Anderson, didn't you go to Pebblebrook High School?" His thought process might be, "How does she know that, did she graduate with me?" Basically, let him tell you his life story. For you internet daters, hitting your crush up on a social website more than once is definitely a no-go. That's just like calling too much; chill out and find a hobby.

4. *Would you seriously date a "one-night stand?"*

This question had different responses that were circumstantial, so for you ladies that took that back rub even though I told you not to; there may be hope in dating your crush. Some guys didn't mind taking it to the next level in a relationship with a girl that they had a one-night stand with because they don't put a "time limit" on sex. One guy actually had a relationship with a one-night stand, but that relationship lasted all of two months; so that was pretty much a waste of time and energy. Other guys were adamant that they would not date a one-night stand. They mentioned that a one-night stand is someone that you have a physical attraction to for that one night and they would wonder if this was the first time she did this. Ladies, a lot of guys like a chase and they enjoy the mystery in getting to know you. If you give them want they want in advance, chances are they won't stick around that long.

When asked if they would reconsider dating the one-night stand if afterwards they took the time out to get to know her. Most stated that it depends on if the girl was actually a good girl and she was not known to be promiscuous. One guy stated that he would not consider the girl "wife material," but he would continue to sleep with her if she had a nice personality. Mind you, all of these guys were single when interviewed so that should let you know that the chances of a one-night stand becoming a long-term relationship are probably slim.

5. *What are the perks of being an Athlete or Greek?*

Now ladies, there are many perks for these guys, but it's females that are the reason behind the perks! Just about all the guys interviewed mentioned that girls cooked, cleaned, did laundry, did their homework, typed their essays, and did their projects. One chick went so far as to attend a group meeting to complete a dude's group project. Please do not be that girl, unless you are going to get a dual degree (your degree and his degree); you need to back up fifty feet from his class syllabi.

One guy made a good point that some of the girls that do these things just want to have the guys name in their mouth. Some chicks are name droppers and like to mention the name of the popular guy on campus in association with them. Even if she is saying, "Girl last night I went to (popular guy's name) place and made a five foot volcano out of popsicle sticks and Elmer's glue for his art project, I think (popular guy's name) likes me." Ladies, you should not feel the need to be subservient just to be around some dude and his social circle. If you generally just want to help out your friend...help him study in the library. Leave all that other foolishness for the chicks that don't know any better because they didn't read my book!

6. *What is your stance on a serious relationship?*

Some of these guys really want to get into a serious relationship but since there are so many girls that throw themselves at them, they have become too picky when choosing a girlfriend. However, majority of the guys who were embarking on their junior or senior year of college were more willing to settle down because of their growth of maturity since their freshmen year. One guy stated that by his junior year of college he was tired of dating random chicks and he just wanted to be with one girl. The whole maturity growth answer was pretty consistent with a lot of the guys interviewed.

Most of the younger guys interviewed looked at me sideways when I mentioned the word "serious relationship," it pretty much wasn't for them. Some of the guys had reasons for not wanting to be in a relationship which included, focusing on their future with no distractions, too young to get serious, not knowing who wants to date them because of their fraternity or athletic affiliations, and just flat out not being interested.

7. *Have you cheated on your girlfriend since you've been in college?*

Well, surprisingly a lot of guys stated that they have not cheated on their girlfriends…well at least they told me they didn't cheat. One guy mentioned that the pressure of so many chicks throwing themselves at him influenced his decision to break-up with his girlfriend. He didn't want to cheat on her but he knew that he wanted to experience college as a free man. A few guys mentioned that they cheated on their girlfriends because it was hard to maintain a monogamous relationship with their chicks in another state. Even though many of the guys interviewed stated that they've never cheated on their girlfriends, a lot of them mentioned that their homeboys cheated in their relationships…feel free to read that with a side-eye.

8. *What type of personality catches your eye?*

This response varied somewhat but the one common thread between all the responses is that guys dig intelligent chicks! I guess so, since the intelligent girls are the ones' doing their homework; just a thought. Many of the guys stated that they like the quiet types that are reserved but still sociable. A lot of dudes stated that they were not really into girls that were always on the scene (always at a party). At the end of the day it's not about the girl that is at all the parties, because partying becomes a hobby in college, it's that one chick at the party that has dance fever and has managed to dance up on every dude at the party like she is in her own competition to be the dancehall queen.

A lot of guys stated that they are attracted to a girl that is down to earth, carries herself with class, and cool enough to chill with. Hey, if you're lucky he might bring you home to momma. Some guys stated that they like girls that "know how to stay in their lane." From a guy's stand point this basically means that if you are not in a relationship with him, you don't call him out about his whereabouts or whose dorm room he was in last night. If the two of you are not in a relationship, neither one of you are in the place to question each other because all-in-all, you two are not in a monogamous relationship... or any relationship at that.

9. *Do Athletes and Greeks kiss and tell?*

YES!!! Ladies please refrain from being the topic of locker room or fraternity meeting conversation because stories are shared. No matter how big your school is, guys talk. Just because they don't make mention that they know about you I am pretty sure they know. He probably won't bring up what he knows about you until you decide that you want to be in a relationship with him. Some guys mentioned that guys don't sit around talking about girls the same way girls sit around talking endlessly about guys; but, they do say enough to where the particulars are known.

PARTIES, CLUBS, AND V.I.P.

*I*f you were brought up in a household like me, the only "parties" you went to your senior year of high school was the homecoming dance and the prom. For some of you, your party life may have been much more alive than mine. Either way it goes, your parents are no longer going to be able to tell you that you can't go to a party because there are going to be booze, boys, and no parental chaperones. This part of college is called being smart, but not academic smart but common sense smart.

During the beginning days of being on campus, after you've unpacked that last box full of clothes you may hear about parties being thrown. Some of these parties may be on campus while other parties are off campus and the party promoter has provided a charter bus to ship you and the other car-less students to the party. Regardless of which parties you choose, make sure you travel in packs or at least with one other female. When I was in college my girls and I had a saying, "If we came together, we leave together." We made sure that everybody we went to a party with left with us too. This is so imperative for having a safe night so that one of your friends does not decide to up and leave with some weird dude. Another pointer for being safe is to never walk alone at night. Don't think that just because you carry around pepper spray you are supernatural and you're not vulnerable to acts of crime.

BLAME IT ON THE ALCOHOL

The parties that are on campus are generally "dry" parties. The word "dry" refers to there being no alcoholic beverages given or sold at the party. I know that many of you ladies are probably under the age of legal alcohol assumption. At the same time I am not naive and I know that many of you will experience your first hangover before you reach the age of twenty-one. I want you to know the dangers of drinking alcohol whether you are under or over the age of twenty-one.

When you consume your first drink you may not feel an alcohol induced buzz. So, you might guzzle another alcoholic beverage down thinking that the first drink didn't do the trick. Well, in all actuality that first drink was working but your brain just didn't distort your sense of functioning just yet for you to feel it. The effects of alcohol consumption can have you feeling as happy as a kid on Christmas Eve and then after a couple of more drinks you may feel as sick as a dog. Before you reach the state of feeling sick as a dog, your hormones may get the best of you and this might be when "drunk dialing" and "drunk texting" take place; and when those forbidden hook-ups go down. You will not remember half of anything you said to that cute guy you've been crushing on if you talk to him while you're intoxicated. Not only will you not remember, but it's quite possible you will make a complete fool of yourself.

You might find that when you've reached the point of drunkenness, your drunken eyes will make any guy that is halfway decent the finest dude at the party. The aftermath of this feeling, depending on how you act on it, can be regrettable to say the least. You might not know it yet, but liquor can give you the "Incredible Strongman Effect." When you are sober you are a regular person, but once you drink that liquid courage you are ready to fight anybody that looks at you the wrong way. After you go through the highs and lows of getting drunk, you may wake up to a hangover (your body is dehydrated) and you may feel like crap for the remainder of the day. With that being said, don't drink and just wait until you are twenty-one to make that decision.

HOUSE PARTIES

House parties may be in a fraternity/sorority house or in a house somewhere off campus. The house parties that are held off campus in a residential community are probably bound to end abruptly by the local police department. So, when attending these parties try not to get too comfortable and be prepared to break in your running shoes. Okay, it may not be that serious where you are breaking out the fifty yard dash, but it probably will be crashed by the cops due to the party being a neighborhood disturbance.

With these parties alcohol is generally given out and no one is carded before being given a drink. Whether you are sipping on a cup of water or a cup of tequila, always watch your cup. Date rape drugs and other tranquilizing drugs are serious and will have you waking up not knowing how you ended up half dressed from the waist down; since these drugs are generally used to better assist someone to commit sexual assault. Some of the effects of these drugs are nausea, dream-like feeling, distorted vision, loss of coordination, slurred speech, and sometimes death. They generally have no taste or smell; so you won't know that you've been given the drug until you are unconscious and clearly by then it's too late. If you or someone you know may have been subject to a date rape drug, call the police immediately and seek medical help.

CLUB TRANSPORTATION

The parties that provide transportation to the club typically provide transportation from the club, but on their time. Make sure you listen out for the DJ to say last call for the shuttle bus or make it a point to know when the last bus will leave. If you miss the last bus, you are going to be stuck between a rock and a hard place wondering how you are going to get back to campus. When I was a freshman in college, my friends and I missed the last call for the shuttle and had to catch a cab back to campus. Lucky for us, we had money to pay for the cab so we got back to campus safely. Needless to say that after that experience we decided to drive to the off campus parties. We just made sure we beat the shuttle buses there because getting in line behind fifty plus students getting off of a bus was a no-go.

THE CLUB SCENE

I know you have seen numerous music videos and movies with a club scene, but let me go ahead and tell you that those club scenes are probably not going to be typical of what you are going to see and experience. Since most of you are under twenty-one reading my book, the lavishness of the club may be the bare minimum to say the least for an eighteen and older club. Clubs are typically hot, and I mean hot as in your edges may sweat out if you are not careful. So the images that you see of the chick in the music video dancing in the club without something as little as a bead of sweat on her forehead is a false illusion and rarely exist in a club if it's packed to capacity. Clubs are crowded if it's popular and may be smoke filled whether done by a smoke machine or people smoking. For you ladies that can't stand the thought of dancing in a club there are places to sit, but the availability of seating is generally limited. It is a nightclub so they do expect you to bust a dance move at some point during the night.

Since the clubs you will be attending are eighteen and older, wristbands are generally given to people that are over twenty-one. When I was under the age of twenty-one, I always questioned the motives of the guys that approached me wearing the twenty-one and older wristband. I could never fathom why a person older than twenty-one would want to party with a bunch of underage college students. But, I'm pretty sure us underage chicks were probably what those older guys were preying on. Be leery of these dudes, because they are technically grown by law but still choose to party with girls that are not legally grown.

CLUB ATTIRE

For some of you ladies that have never set foot in a night club you are probably wondering what you should wear. The clothes worn at eighteen and older clubs varies because some of you are into different styles of dress. Teen clubs typically do not have a dress code of any sort so you might see a chick that has on sneakers, a denim mini-skirt, and a white tank standing next to a chick wearing a spandex dress with some heels. Regardless of what you wear, you are probably going to sweat in it so be mindful of that when picking out something to wear.

Wear what you feel comfortable in and don't mind standing in for a long period of time. For you ladies that want to rock your freshest pair of sneakers to the club, I am going to tell you in advance that your sneakers might not be so fresh when you leave the club. Clubs are typically packed and when you navigate through the club you might get drinks spilled on your sneakers and people will probably step on them as well.

V.I.P.

Once you are in the club you may notice the VIP area. This area is usually sectioned off and provides a comfortable atmosphere that is supposed to be like having your own private party at the club. Depending on the club set up this area may be along the walls of the club or elevated somewhere in the club. People generally pay to party in this area, whether they paid for a table or they paid for a wristband. This area usually has seating and tables set up in some kind of uniform fashion; hey, you gotta put those champagne bottles somewhere. Let me inform you about a couple of things pertaining to this area.

Some guys feel as though they are doing you a favor by bringing you over to their VIP section, but you were probably fine where you were at. If a dude gets beyond himself and starts acting reckless, leave his section; you are in VIP now, just walk around and enjoy the rest of the night. If you don't have a wristband; make sure the security staff by the entrance of the VIP area sees your face so you can come and go out of this area as you please.

If you glance over at this area and there is a table full of eight dudes, please know that all eight of them probably chipped in money to reserve the section. Don't believe the hype and think that just because a dude brings you and your homegirls to his section that he is about something. This type of guy probably thinks that being in that section will give you the illusion that his cubic zirconium necklace, medallion, pinkie ring, bracelet, and the bezel on his watch are real diamonds; and that his album is really going to drop in three months. This guy might buy you and all your friends' drinks like money is not an issue. Well, money might not be an issue that night but that bar tab is.

Some clubs include a fee for drinks when someone purchases a table in VIP…you can't drink tap water at the table all night. So, you may be invited into some random dudes table and he might tell you and your girls to order whatever you like, and in the back of your mind you might think this dude is ballin' out of control. No boo, he is really trying to run out that $200 liquor tab that was included with his table and get you comfortably drunk in the process.

"LET ME BUY YOU A DRINK"

This brings me to another club warning; there are guys that will be chummy with you the whole night in the club and buy you as many drinks as you like. He probably thinks that if you hang out with him the whole time and he keeps a drink in your hand, you will start to "trust" him and think that you know him. By the end of the night the club lights let up and you are wasted (drunk), this would be the opportune time for him to mention how you should come back to his place tonight and for your intoxicated mind to agree. This is why you should always stick with the friends that you came to the club with. If you meet a great guy in the club speak to him, maybe exchange numbers and keep it moving. You came to the club to have fun with your friends, not with some random guy you just met…he is technically a stranger.

DANCING IN THE CLUB

For you ladies out there that have never been to an un-chaperoned party, the dance floor may be a totally new scene for you. There is not going to be someone breaking up people grinding on the dance floor because they are dancing too close. I know that you may love to dance and you might have won a few dance contests in your day but be respectful of yourself. Just because you know how to drop into a split at any given moment doesn't mean you should do it in the club; as a matter of fact, never drop into a split at the club.

On a side note, if a club has a stage that does not mean that the stage is meant for you to dance on. Please know that the stage is probably meant for live performances and your dancing should not be that live performance. You may see chicks on stage dancing or even on the bar dancing but not in a way that is befitting of a young lady; trust, people may be looking at these chicks but those looks are probably glares. Please do not be one of those chicks dancing on the stage, bar, table top or any other flat surface that's not the main dance floor.

When dancing know what you are comfortable with and don't let some dude touch you in a way that makes you feel uncomfortable. Most guys want to dance behind you and if you make it a point to dance face-to-face they will probably position themselves so that the dance becomes more of mating dance. If a guy makes you feel uncomfortable at anytime when you are dancing with him, walk away from him and if he is seriously making you feel uncomfortable tell security. When dancing please don't be that chick in the club that looks like she is about to conceive a child on the dance floor. That is so not the business; there is a difference between dancing on the dance floor and fornicating on the dance floor. But then again, you are reading my book so I know chances are slim you are going to be that chick.

Don't forget…

- Being the last person to leave a party or a club is not the person you want to be; this is not a good look.

- If you and your girls came together, you and your girls need to leave together.
- Club security and bouncers are your friends, well the friends you want to have in the club.
- VIP is not all that it is cracked up to be and sometimes it is more crowded than the rest of the club; some private party within a party.
- Don't let your friends encourage you to dance on top of a bar, stage, table, club furniture, or a dude.
- Always be observant of your surroundings because you would not want to be the bystander that got caught up in an alcohol induced fight.
- Don't give your phone number to every dude that speaks to you and tells you that you should be a model.

SEX: UN-CHAPERONED

*A*s much as I want to believe that you will keep your chastity belt on lock at all times, I know that you are human and you might partake in sexual acts of some form or fashion. One thing I must say is; be a lady about the situation...a smart lady at that. Always, and I repeat always, make sure your guy is wearing a condom and if you wear female condoms make sure you are wearing one of those too. Some college chicks mentioned to me that when they started going to college, they just starting carrying condoms in their purses just in case their private study session ended with a bang. I know some of you reading this may think that only promiscuous chicks carry around male condoms, but I guarantee you that you would much rather be a smart promiscuous chick who comes prepared with a condom than a chick with a burning vaginal area.

For some of you, you will be embarking college as a virgin. My advice to you is to keep your virginity throughout college until you get married. I know it may seem hard but it can be done; I know of females that have withstood from having sex during college and are still virgins till this day. Just to feel you in, sex is not what the Hollywood movies make it out to be. I doubt if there will be candles lit everywhere and I seriously doubt that everything is going to happen in slow motion with your favorite love song playing in the background. So, in all actuality you are really not missing out on much. There are men that value a female that has chosen to withstand from sexual acts until they are married. Ultimately, the choice is yours to make so make it wisely.

For some of my more sexually advanced readers, there is a major change in sexual relationships in college than there was when you were in high school. That major change is the fact that you have the freedom to have sex whenever you want and you no longer have to sneak around your parents to have sex. With this freedom comes much responsibility that should be acknowledged. On a side note, some freshman dorms have visitation hours so don't take the term "whenever" too loosely.

Ladies, there is an old saying that states, "What happens in the dark will come to light." This means that the things you do in private will somehow reveal themselves. As I have mentioned before, guys talk and what you did in private last night may not be private for that long; I'm pretty sure you will tell a friend and he will tell a friend. If you choose to have unprotected sex with dudes in private, the results of your decision may reveal itself as an embryo or a colony of blisters.

WE HAD SEX, I THINK HE LIKES ME

Some of you might be living in a fairytale world and you're probably under the impression that sex with a guy equates to a relationship. Well, I'm sorry sweetie but in the real world sex with a guy equates to just that….sex with a guy. You could end up being in a situation where you like a guy and you might think that by you having sex with him it will show him that you really like him. After you have sex with him you may be stuck wondering whether he is going to call you or if things between the two of you are going to be awkward.

One thing you will come to notice is that sex means something different to different people. You may view sex as something sacred shared between two married people, while someone else may view sex as something that pleases them. If you are going to engage in sexual activities of any kind know that it may come with some emotional consequences. Some of these emotional consequences include guilt and mixed feelings about the guy, how you feel about yourself and the decision you made to have sex.

With this being said, sex can make things complicated with a guy that you are not in a relationship with. Just because you decide to have sex with a dude on your campus it doesn't mean that he is now your boyfriend. If the two of you are not in a relationship don't be surprised to see the dude that had your mind blown the night before walking around campus with his arm around some other chick. If there is no monogamous commitment there is no relationship. For the record, "just talking" is not a relationship title; that's just a nice way of saying friends with benefits. The whole time you think that the two of you are working towards a "relationship" he just wants to keep you on the "homie, lover, friend" status. Don't play yourself and fall for this title, it's pointless and leads you absolutely nowhere.

BECOME ONE WITH YOUR BODY

You should really get to know your body and its natural odors so you will know when something is not right with your vaginal area. If you notice something irregular you should go to the campus clinic (your tuition pays for it whether or not you ever step foot in there) and schedule an appointment. If you are insecure about sitting in the campus clinic because, "you don't want everybody in your business" please take your exclusive self down to the nearest clinic. Make sure you call and set up an appointment and check to see what documentations you might need to bring. Never ignore your bodies warning signals because something far worse could be lurking in the midst.

For you ladies that are considering engaging in some form of sexual act, you might want to consider a form of birth control. Please be mindful that birth control is not an excuse to let your dude go comdomless. Birth control helps prevent the conception of a child, not the conception of an STD. If you catch yourself in a condom-less situation, I recommend that you run to the nearest clinic within 3 months of contact to get tested for HIV and all other STD's. Below is a list of STD's that have symptoms and even though you might not experience any symptoms of any kind, you should still go to the gynecologist once a year or more depending on your sexual lifestyle. Since I care for the well being of your sexual health I took the time to provide you with some information from the Department of Health and Human Services: Centers for Disease Control and Prevention (CDC).

HPV:
There are over 100 types of the Human Papilloma Virus and high-risk HPV can cause cervical cancer. It can be spread through anal sex, vaginal sex, and skin-to-skin contact with body rubbing. Regular Pap smears are important to detect any cell changes before cancer forms with a cervical cancer screening. When you go to a gynecologist you should request to take an HPV test. Most HPV infections go away within 8-13 months but some don't and they hide in your body. It can affect the scrotum, rectum, vagina, cervix, anus, vulva, and the penis. **Symptoms:** Genital warts in the form of small bumps or groups of bumps, cervical cancer, and cancer of the anus, vulva, vagina, and penis.

Vaccine: Three injections can be given to you during the course of 6 months and can prevent two types of the HPV virus that causes 70% of cervical cancer cases and two types of HPV that causes 90% of genital warts cases.

Treatment: There is no cure because most types of HPV are harmless but if precancerous cell changes occur, abnormal tissues have to be removed either by cryotherapy (frozen off), laser surgery, or leep (thin wire loop uses electrical current to remove abnormal tissue).

GONORRHEA

Can cause pelvic inflammatory disease if untreated which can damage the fallopian tubes and cause infertility. It can infect the penis, cervix, vagina, anus, urethra, and throat. The highest reported rates of infection are among sexually active teenagers and young adults.

Symptoms: Painful urination and painful intercourse, yellowish or yellow green discharge, increased vaginal discharge, and irregular menstrual bleeding between menstrual cycles; however, many people have no symptoms at all.

Treatment: Antibiotics eradicate the gonorrhea bacteria.

HERPES

There are two different herpes viruses. One is Herpes Simplex Virus 1, which is oral and common. It can be found in cold sores and fever blisters on the lips and around the mouth. This type is harmless and can be found in children and adults.

The other type is Herpes Simplex Virus 2; it is more common in women (one out of four) and less common in men (one out of eight). It's found in the genital area, vagina, penis, anus, cervix, and the buttocks. It causes outbreaks of blisters on or around the genitals and rectum. These outbreaks leave sores that can last up to two to four weeks. The numbers of outbreaks may decrease over time. Both of these types of herpes remain in the body for life and are passed through brief skin-to-skin contact, oral, vaginal, and anal sex; the symptoms come and go.

Symptoms: The symptoms for Herpes Simplex Virus 2 are blisters, open sores, painful urination when urine passes over sores, cluster of blister sores, flu-like illness, backache, fever, and swollen glands.

Treatment: There is no cure for herpes but there are drugs that speed up the healing of sores and help prevent future outbreaks.

TRICHOMONIASIS

This is the most common curable STD in young women; there are around 7.4 million new cases every year. It is a vaginal infection that is spread through contact with surfaces containing infected secretions such as penis-to-vagina sexual contact and vulva-to-vulva contact with someone who is infected.

Symptoms: Unpleasant smell in discharge, a frothy yellow-green discharge, painful urination, and sexual discomfort.

Treatment: Prescription drugs by mouth or single dose.

BACTERIAL VAGINOSIS

Also known as "BV," it is caused by a change in the balance of different kinds of bacteria in the vagina and it is not always caused by sexual contact. Your vagina contains good bacteria and damaging bacteria and the BV develops when there are more damaging bacteria than good bacteria.

Symptoms: Vaginal odor, vaginal discharge with a strong unpleasant odor, pain, and itching; however, many women have no symptoms.

Treatment: Antibiotics and antimicrobial creams.

CHLAMYDIA

It is common and an invisible transmitted bacterial infection that can damage a woman's reproductive organs if left untreated. The damage to the reproductive organs can be irreversible and cause infertility. If Chlamydia is left untreated it can lead to Pelvic Inflammatory Disease (PID) which can damage the fallopian tubes, uterus, and surrounding tissue.

Symptoms: It can cause painful urination, abdominal pain, abnormal discharge, painful sex, and lower back pain. It is known as being "silent" because three quarters of infected women and around half of men have no symptoms.

Treatment: Antibiotics destroy the Chlamydia bacteria.

PUBIC LICE

Also known as "crabs," it is spread through sexual contact. It's hardly ever spread through bed linens, towels, clothes or by sitting on toilet seat because lice can not live far away from a human body. It is known as "crabs" because under a magnifying glass they look like tiny crabs. They are tan or grayish-white in color and they feed off of blood.

Symptoms: Intense itching in the genital area or anus.

Treatment: Over the counter lice killing lotion, shampoo or mousse like A200, InnoGel Plus, and RID.

HIV

Also known as the Human Immunodeficiency Virus that causes AIDS. It breaks down the immune system and causes the body to breakdown because of something as simple as the common cold. Your immune system fights off infections and HIV attacks the immune system. It is transmitted through blood, semen, vaginal fluid, infected needles, breast feeding, and sex. It is can be spread through anal, vaginal, and oral sex (with oral sex it can be spread if you have open sores in your mouth). This disease can not be spread through sharing a drinking fountain, misquotes, shaking hands, casual kissing, and other general day-to-day activities.

Symptoms: There are not really any definitive symptoms for HIV because many people that are infected live years without knowing. The only way to know if you are infected with HIV is to get tested.

Know This: Once your body is infected with the disease your body produces antibodies and most HIV test looks for these antibodies. When wondering when to get tested after a possible exposure to the disease, most people will have detectable antibodies within two to eight weeks after the initial exposure. You should also consider getting tested 3 months following the exposure because ninety-seven percent of people infected developed antibodies during this time. In rare cases it can take up to 6 months to develop HIV antibodies. There are new ways of getting tested for HIV and you will know the results the same day that you are tested. These tests can require something as simple as oral fluid, urine, or a finger-stick of blood to test you for HIV. If you ever need to find a testing site you can call the CDC-INFO at 1-800-232-4636. You can call this number 24 hours a day and it is confidential or you can visit the National HIV Testing Resource website at http://www.hivtest.org

Treatment: There is not a cure but there are treatments and medicine that can help a person live longer with the virus.

Ladies, be mindful of your actions and always remember that it is imperative to keep yourself healthy and if you are going to have sex; have protected sex. I always say; "A Healthy Vagina is a Happy Vagina." All of these STD's that I mentioned can be transmitted through unprotected sex and I didn't even mention everything that can be transmitted through unprotected sex. So that should just let you know that not wearing a condom during sex is never a good look. I don't care how fine he is or how clean he looks, just because he doesn't have blisters on his genital area does not mean that there is nothing prowling in the midst…..STD'S do not discriminate.

If you want to avoid this all together practice abstinence or celibacy and if the dude you are feeling doesn't appreciate your decision to abstain from sex, chuck those deuces because he isn't the right dude for you. If you have any questions or need facts about sexual transmitted diseases you should reference sites like The Centers for Disease Control and Prevention. Never and I mean NEVER try to self-diagnose yourself by looking at possible symptoms. The only way to officially know that you are infected with an STD is to get tested.

A Pledge to Myself…

I, _____, pledge to never engage in any sexual activity without the use of a condom. I pledge to visit the gynecologist at least once a year and not fear or ignore any abnormalities that may occur in my vaginal area. As I am now aware of some of the STD's and HIV/AIDS, I vow to protect myself and abstain from sexual intercourse if a condom is not available. I have acknowledged that to love myself I must protect myself, and to protect myself I must make sure a condom is always used to prevent the spread of venereal diseases.

(Signature) _____

(Date) _____

HEY, I THINK I'M PREGNANT

After I wrote this chapter some friends of mine read it and had mix feelings. Some felt as though I shouldn't add this chapter because it is a sensitive subject and others felt that since I was including this chapter I was condoning teenage pregnancy. This is what I will tell you and what I told them, "I am not encouraging teenage girls to run out and get pregnant while in college, but the truth of the matter is teenage girls are having children while in high school. So it wouldn't be right for me not to mention this subject because it can inspire those that either have a child prior to college or become pregnant while in college and let them know that getting a college degree is possible with child."

-Lakisha Henderson

*L*et's say hypothetically you have a boyfriend in college, and in the back of your mind he is the guy that you dream of starting a family with someday. Now, let's say that "someday" happens to come your junior year of college. There may be a lot of things running through your mind, more like your life flashing before your eyes. At first your family might not be the happiest campers to hear that their daughter is pregnant but what's done is done, and all they can do is accept the fact that you are an adult that made an adult decision. If you end up getting pregnant in college I want you to know that your dreams of graduating college are not over.

Throughout your college career you may see females that become pregnant, but you will also notice how many of these females don't give up and still manage to graduate. This is a new day in age and there are ways to attend school and maintain the role of mother to your child. Although having a child while in college may require outside assistance and a great support system, your dreams of graduating are obtainable; it is just going to take more work to get it done. You probably won't be able to drop it like it's hot at the club with all of your friends for a while; since you are preggers and all. You are really going to have to buckle down and focus on your college education because now you have another mouth to feed.

BEFORE THE BABY

There are educational options you can take if you do get pregnant while in college. You can consider taking classes over the internet; this can be great when you are further along in your pregnancy and your mobility is limited due to that bun in the oven. Another thing you can consider is independent study, with independent study you and a faculty member will agree on a topic and meet periodically to check on your progress. Since you are going to need to take some time off due to your pregnancy, you should look into summer semesters and mini-semesters (between spring and summer semester) if offered. You should meet with your academic advisor as to how you can arrange your classes around your pregnancy. Some colleges have day care centers for children of staff, faculty, and students that attend the college. Check to see if there is a subsidized rate for childcare since you are a college student.

One female I know had a child her junior year of college and she mentioned to me how her life changed. She matured a great deal and her social life changed a bit since her friends still frequented the clubs. She mentioned that once her pregnancy began to show, people were shocked that she was pregnant. But she didn't take their shock as something she should be ashamed of. At the end of the day she knew that she had a blessing in her body that she was going to take care of.

AFTER THE BABY

She mentioned that the actual pregnancy was easy while attending school because the only thing that changed was the fact that she no longer sat at a desk and instead sat at a table while in class. It was after she had her baby that she realized how much stronger she was going to have to be to stay in college. She knew it would have been easy for her to sit out a semester, but she was determined to finish college with her graduating class. She depended a lot on her family and the baby's father's family for support. She scheduled her classes in a way that allowed her to watch her baby mostly during the day and attend classes later in the evening. There was a sense of teamwork with everyone involved in helping her raise her child and graduate from college. There were many nights that she cried wanting to give up on graduating and just be a stay at home mother and discontinue her college education. Instead, she focused that energy on her dream and she graduated with her class.

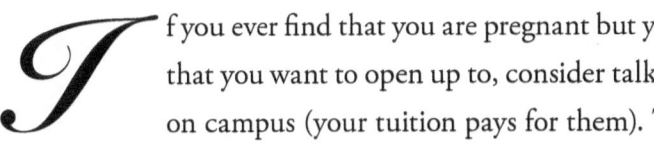 f you ever find that you are pregnant but you don't have anyone that you want to open up to, consider talking to the counselors on campus (your tuition pays for them). These counselors can

give you insight on your situation. There are pregnancy hotlines you can call for comfort; they are generally free of charge, 24/7 and confidential. When deciding what the future outcome of your pregnancy will be, never factor in the thought, "what will everyone think of me?" At the end of the day you will have to live with the decisions you make.

FRIENDS OR FOE

*I*f you were like me, you grew up as a child watching sitcoms and movies pertaining to college life. This was my only glimpse growing up on what college life was like; although very PG, I honestly thought college life was like a sitcom filled with a close knit of five or more friends, mild drama, and a couple of comedic punch lines here and there. In all actuality, this may be the scenario for your college experience, so don't think that your college life has to be a sequel to your drama filled high school life.

However, while I was in college I realized that my college experience didn't add up to what I saw on television. I, not being the social butterfly type nor did I blossom into one, pretty much just kept close to one or two people max and if you saw one of us on campus you saw the other. Don't get me wrong, I knew a lot of people and met great people along the way but I just didn't get too close to everybody to the point where we all would hang out daily or share personal secrets...the latter part was definitely not going down on my end. I had many friends in college but I only had one or two close friends that I would call on if I needed any advice; I didn't want you to think that I had some weird social issues or anything.

College is the time to form everlasting friendships since you're probably going to shed some of your high school friends once you graduate. If you are reading this before your graduation, I'm sorry to tell you that you might not keep in touch with all five hundred plus students that graduated with you. You are about to embark on the time of your life where the people that are about to be your friends are not necessarily from your hometown; some of them were probably a bore anyway.

I suggest that you be open-minded when making friendships with people at your college. This will be a wonderful time where you can experience other cultures socially. You might not have been friends with anybody outside of your race or financial bracket due to your schools' demographics. Take advantage of this time of meeting people from different backgrounds and cultivate yourself.

THE FRIENDS

All friendships are not going to be cheery and gleeful and you should know that every girl you meet is not destined to be your BFF. You might quite naturally hang out with people that share a common interest as you. For example, if you are apart of an organization like the marching band or the debate team while you are in college the people in these organizations might be the people you form the strongest bonds with because you are around them so much. You may also form friendships with people within your major through classes; you never know, the friendship could flourish into a business partnership.

You should take pictures with your new college buds like you are the paparazzi and post it on social networking sites (don't act like you don't already do it) and live it up with your new friends in college. These photos will be a constant reminder of the good times had by you and your friends. On a side note, please be cautious of the photos you post on social networking sites. If you ever have to think, "Wow, I hope this picture doesn't come back to bite me in the butt later in life when I am running for Congress," don't post it. Pictures posted on the internet can have a longer life on the internet even after you delete the picture from your profile. With the magical tool of cut and paste, it will take a lot more than a shredder to never see those pictures resurface later on in life.

Whomever you find yourself socializing with the most at the start of college, just know that you have known them for all of let's say three months. So don't be an open book and let them know every detail of your life. Quite frankly, if your life is filled with a thousand amazing stories, write a book. You might want to fall back from indulging all of your deep dark secrets to your new college friends. It probably took you years to determine who your best friends were in high school, so don't think that the first girl you meet in college is going to instantly be your new best friend.

Just think of how long it took for you to build up trust with your friends from back home, the same should apply to your new college friends. Once you deem your new friends loyal of knowing that you secretly have a crush on a guy in one of your classes pinky promise and tell. But until then, keep those personal secrets between you, your diary, and your best buds from back home.

Dear Keesh,

I've been hanging out with this hot guy that I've been crushing on in my Psychology class and I told this girl that I'm cool with. The next thing I know, I hear that she is hanging out with him and those two are an item. I thought she was my true friend and would never go behind my back and get at the guy that I've been daydreaming about for the last two months. Where did I go wrong?

- A Homegirl Scarred

For starters you shouldn't go around advertising how breath-taking some guy is to a "friend" that you just met; that's where you went wrong. You have to realize that some chicks may be curious and will see if what you say is true. You never know, her motto might be: "It ain't no fun if the hommies can't get none." I would suggest that you keep those juicy details about your crush to yourself or if you find yourself busting out the seams wanting to tell someone, tell your BFF from back at home.

-Keesh

THE FOE

There are some reasons why I am telling you not to go full throttle into best friends' mode with every girl that you hold a decent conversation with. One reason is because unlike in high school, the new girls you meet are not always going to be genuine with you. This is pretty much how the real world is so you might as well get used to it now. In high school, your best buds may have been people that you have known since elementary. Since you guys have known each other for so long there is loyalty between all of you. Please don't think that I don't want you to make new friends, just be leery of whom you let into your personal space because quite frankly, some people are trifling when it comes to friendships.

Imagine this, you attend college and you meet a girl. Let's say she lives in your dorm and during your first semester at school the two of you become the best of buds. Soon after you start to open up to her a bit about your life, then the stories about your life turns into you telling her secrets about your personal life. Don't see this whole pinkie promise secret telling session as a problem, eh? Well, eventually this friend and you may fall out (terminate your friendship) over something as silly as a guy or something dealing with loyalty in the friendship. Guess what? Now she knows things about you that were only meant for her to know.

Well, since you really couldn't conduct a background check upon meeting her, you might have been unaware of her trifling past with friendships. So, with this being said she could decide to tell anybody that will listen all of your dirty little secrets. FYI, college is the same as high school in the spirit of rumors. So you might want to jot down those secrets in your mental journal. Hopefully you never encounter "the foe," I just wanted to keep you on your toes and let you know that all friendships are not magical.

THE BESTIE'S (BESTFREINDS)

Make sure you surround yourself with awesome people and remember to treat people how you want to be treated. The people you consider your friends should motivate you to be a better person inside and out. They should encourage you to make great choices in life. If you feel as though one of your friends is sucking the joy out of your life tell them to exit stage left. You will meet a lot of people and form many friendships but the one's that you keep near and dear to your heart are your true friends.

Another thing when choosing your close friends, know that they are a reflection of you. You may have a lot of friends on campus but there will be a select few of whom you hang out with on the daily. The people you hang out with on the daily are the people that are going to be that reflection of you. There is an old saying that, "Birds of a feather flock together." This saying may not be accurate in judging all social cliques but people may view you by the people you hang with.

For instance, let's say that you hang out with a group of girls that party hard and on occasion hold the private after party in their dorm rooms. In all actuality, you are the designated purse holder at all the parties and you have never let a boy up in your room for a private after party of any kind. Regardless of this, people don't see you, they see the people you associate yourself with as the person you are. So, be mindful of the company you keep!

Things you shouldn't do for your new college friends...

1. Do not co-sign on anything or put something in your name (your line of credit) for a friend. When I say the word "something," I mean anything that requires a monthly payment. This is a great way to start the process of bad credit, especially when your new friend does not uphold their end of the bargain and pay the bill on time...or ever.

2. Do not decide to become roommates off campus sophomore year (when you can live on campus) if this new friend is always talking about how broke she is. Why would you want to sign a lease with her? You will be setting yourself up for an eviction notice.

3. Do not extend a personal loan (cash or credit) to a friend because chances are you will be kissing that money goodbye longer than you think. Is it really paying you back when you get the money back two years later? Unless you can do without those funds for an extended amount of time, don't lend out your money... instead lend out some advice and tell your friend to get a job.

4. Do not give out your credit cards, social security number, or the PIN number for your debit card to a friend. This is a no-brainer; if you decide to lend out your social security number you may find out later in life that you have a twin you never knew about...a twin called "Identity Fraud." Lending out your PIN number or your credit cards to an untrustworthy friend will just leave you broke.

5. Do not let a friend borrow your favorite sweater or the beloved pearls your grandmother gave you on your 16th birthday. If you would pass out at the thought of living without it, know that it is good as gone if you lend it out.

CLASSES

lasses are an important part of college because your academic progress is determined by how well you perform in class. It can be challenging getting used to the independence of going to class because it's so easy to brush class off when you have been out partying the night before. You must set high standards for yourself and know that you came to college with the intent of someday graduating. Therefore, you should avoid procrastination at all cost because procrastination and graduation do not mix. I've set this chapter for things to consider before scheduling classes and ways to pass those classes.

WHAT IS YOUR MAJOR/MINOR?

Some of you will go to college knowing just what your major, minor, and dual degree will be in. Others of you will just be elated to be in college and haven't yet decided what you want to do in life. Don't fret; there are college graduates that still don't know what they want to do in life. For those of you that have not yet declared a major, don't get your panties in a bunch because you have some time to decide. You don't typically have to declare a major until the second semester of your sophomore year of college.

When deciding a major I suggest that you visit the career center for guidance and to review a course catalog. You can consider registering for classes that spark an interest in you and within that department you can see if something in particular motivates you. You may also want to think about subjects that came easily to you in high school and subjects you enjoyed. These are a few things you can do before you have to declare a major so you do not end up trying to change your major during your senior year because you finally decided a career path.

At some point during your first semester I recommend that you make it a point to meet with your academic advisor. This person is there to help you map out your academic college career and point you down the right path to graduate. At some colleges, this person may be more hands on and they may be more accessible whenever you need them. At other colleges, you may have to schedule an appointment two months down the line just to meet with them. Whatever the case may be, get to know your academic advisor and meet with them as often as possible.

SCHEDULING CLASSES

For starters, you need to know your self and whether or not you function better in the morning or in the afternoon. For you early birds out there, you might want to start your classes around 9:00 a.m. or 10:00 a.m. The advantage of starting your classes early is that you are done with your classes sooner and that will leave you more free time in the afternoon. This means that you will have more time to hang out with that cute guy in your English class. For you late risers you might want to consider starting your academic day around 12:00 p.m. or 1:00 p.m. This will give you enough time to sleep in a bit and you will be well rested to attend class.

When registering for classes, which will ultimately determine your daily schedule, you might want to consider a few things. You might want to consider scheduling your classes back-to-back. For instance, if you have a class at 10:00 a.m. you might want to follow that up with a class at 11:00 a.m. Let's say that you have a 9:00 a.m. class (that lasts an hour) followed by a 12:00 p.m. class and you have a two hour gap in between your classes. Are you really going to go back to your dorm room for those two spare hours and take a cat nap? If you have too big of a gap in between your classes, the chances of you attending the last class might be slim to none.

Another thing to consider when scheduling classes is how many classes can you handle in a single day? If you schedule four classes on the same day, please know that you might have four papers due on the same day or four exams on the same day. Professors do not know what other classes you are taking and could care less if they scheduled an exam on the same day that you have another exam. With your classes you may also want to consider its location. I tried to take as many classes in the same buildings, which meant less traveling on campus on my part...especially on rainy days.

THE NOTE TAKER

Since there may be days when your hair looks a mess or you're bloated and you can't make it to class, you may need to make sure you have a "note taker" friend. In every class you need to make a friend that looks very diligent in their note taking or the person that seems to pass every exam with flying colors. This person needs to also have a great class attendance record, because if you don't show up to class they will need to be there taking the notes you should have been taking.

Lakisha Henderson

<u>THE STUDY BUDDY</u>

Another friend you may want to make is the male study buddy; he is cute and the one thing the two of you have in common is that the both of you are in the same class. This can be an excuse to mingle with the guy sitting two rows over that you have been crushing on since the first day of class and a chance for you to get ahead academically. Make sure your study sessions never occur in a dorm room, because the chances of the two of you studying are slim to none...with the distraction of the television and all.

So, you might want to try to study in the library somewhere tucked away where the two of you can focus, or so you can gaze into his eyes without any interruptions. If you are really interested in this guy and you want to create a backdrop for your study session try going to a coffee shop. Coffee shops are sometimes dimly lit and can be quite cozy and can make for a great study session. With any class, you should consider pairing up with people in that class for study sessions before an exam. This is a great way for you to gain different insight on the topic or share study material.

Dear Keesh,

I am having problems studying; I've studied in the library and silently in my dorm room. But no matter how long and hard I study and where I study, I can't seem to retain the information during the exam. What can I try to do to make good use of my study sessions?

Sincerely,
-Perturbed Academic Achiever

I don't think your problem is in where you are studying. Your problem is in your method of retaining information. If you just read through the chapters in your book and review your class notes you probably won't remember much when it counts the most on the day of the exam. You might want to try relating your class information to more personable things so you can enhance your memorization. For instance, if you need to remember that the 21st Constitutional Amendment allowed the legal sales and consumption of liquor after it had been previously prohibited. Just remember that you have to be 21 years old to legally drink liquor which is the same number for the 21st amendment. Basically, just make the material relatable in some way so it will be easier to remember when you are taking an exam.

-Keesh

THE ART OF STUDYING

Studying is a big part of your academic success. It is imperative that you find what works best for you when studying. Some of you may find that it's tortuous to study in a quiet library filled with distractions; the easy access to a nearby eatery was distraction enough for me. Others of you may find that the library is the perfect place for you to study because you can not get that comfortable in there to fall asleep. Some of you may find that studying in your dorm room isn't the perfect place because it's too many real distractions like your bed, television, and computer.

I personally found that studying in my dorm room was perfect; I would just sit up in my bed and study my notes in silence. As I studied my notes, I would highlight information within my notes that I knew I had retained. Therefore, I knew what information I needed to go more in depth on with the textbook because usually it wasn't highlighted and probably had a question mark next to it. Some people can just study from the book but I was big on note taking; that's what helped me pass my classes.

Another way to study is to quiz yourself by using your resources. At the end of each chapter or section of your textbook you may see a summary section. This section is a good resource when studying because there may be a quiz you can take. I recommend that you test yourself with these quizzes; it can help you see just how far off you are from doing a good job on the exam. Another study method that was effective for me involved the use of index cards. I put a definition on one side of the index card and put the answer on the other side. After I studied them, I would quiz myself. I put the index cards that I got right in one pile and the index cards that I got wrong in another pile. Then I would review the index cards I got wrong so next time I quizzed myself they would all be in the pile for answers that were correct.

Acronyms are another great way to study materials that are grouped together. If you need to know the three main parts of the brain you can remember F.H.M., as in FHM Magazine. This represents the Forebrain, Hindbrain, and Midbrain. If you are studying something a bit lengthier than this, make up a long mnemonic. A mnemonic is a set of words put together in a logical arrangement to assist in memorization. Let's say you need to know the major external parts of the human brain. You can remember it with this mnemonic by saying: "Old People Fart Chocolate Tarts." This represents the Olfactory bulb, Pons, Frontal Lobe, Cerebellum, and Temporal Lobes. Any method you decide to use when studying is awesome as long as it works, there is no use studying for an exam and failing that exam. That my friend is nothing but wasted time had by all.

TAKING NOTES

Taking great notes in class is another resource when studying for exams. Notes are imperative when studying because they are in reference to what the professor spoke about in class. If you are in a lecture course, your teacher may talk during the whole class period. I doubt if your professor will stop so that you can catch up because you missed a word or two. I suggest you learn the art of abbreviations and abbreviate some words when taking notes. If taking notes from a lecture seems foreign to you, you might want to consider investing in a good voice recorder. You might look kind of geeky with your voice recorder sitting off the edge of your desk, but hey there is nothing geeky about getting an "A" in class.

The professor's lectures are usually nothing but their notes being verbally read to you, so it would behoove you to listen up. After I took notes from the professor in class, I would take another set of notes from the book that were more in-depth so that I could get a better grasp about what my professor was talking about. I started doing this for one of my harder classes and I passed with flying colors, so I applied this to my easier classes and my exams were a cinch.

This may seem like too much to do for one class, but when you start failing your exams you will know that you are no longer in high school. Some professors' give lectures off of a PowerPoint presentation; this does not give you an excuse not to attend class or not to take notes. Just because you printed out the PowerPoint prior to class you still need to go and take notes from the lecture. You still need to bring a writing utensil, paper, and your book to class. I'm pretty sure your professor will go more in depth about each PowerPoint slide when they give the actual lecture.

GET TO KNOW YOUR PROFESSOR

Ladies, get to know your teacher. This is imperative especially if you need a recommendation or if you need a passing grade. If your class is small this can easily be done. You can speak up in class and ask questions or be active and contribute during class discussions. Its fine to be interested in the class discussion but don't become that one person in class that is overly inquisitive. So for you, "So, what if..." people you might want to write your list of fifty questions down on a piece of paper and meet with your professor in private during their office hours.

Let's say you are in a lecture class that has over one hundred students in it. The chances of you standing out are not that great. These professors might not have great office hours, but their teacher assistants might have office hours. In this case, make sure you know your assigned teacher's assistant and if they schedule a study session make it a point to attend at least one of them.

If you don't make it an effort to speak up in class, go to office hours or attend scheduled study sessions so at least you seem as though you are putting forth the effort to pass the class. You will want to be on good terms with your professors when you need a recommendation for that internship two years from now or for that scholarship that can save you money on your college tuition.

BUY YOUR BOOKS

Ladies, always buy books for class. I know those Paper Denim jeans looked really good and tempting when you tried them on, but buy your books first. You might meet some upperclassmen that may tell you that they never bought a book for class and they still passed the class. Take a second and ask them what they passed the class with, if they tell you they got an "A" in the class chances are they are not telling you the truth; unless they were taking a gym class. Books can be very expensive and once you add up the total for your first semester books, your total may be around five-hundred dollars or more. This is typical and can be expected your first year of school. But, take note because there are ways to cut corners when buying books.

For starters, upperclassmen had the same classes and books that you may need your freshman year and they no longer need them. These upperclassmen generally sell their books for a fraction of the price and you can probably negotiate a cheaper price. Usually when you are moving onto campus there are flyers posted around campus advertising books for sale. Another way to avoid spending so much money is buying your books off the internet. Buying your books this way can save you money but in some cases you are better off buying your books from the school's bookstore. So, make sure you do your homework when buying books and compare prices if you want to save on money that can be spent on something you enjoy. After you buy all of your books for school, make sure you use them which means open them once in a while and take them to class. Since you own the book that you paid $50 for mark it up with a high lighter during class and when taking notes; you might as well now that it is yours.

THE TOUGH PROFESSOR

I know that you may be worried about your professors while you are enrolling into classes because unlike high school, you may have no idea who they are. If you are fortunate to have friends that are already enrolled in the college you are about to attend you might have an upper hand in knowing who is a good professor. Some professors have a reputation for being tough and I really think they pride themselves on that reputation. Unless you love a challenge, this may be the professor you want to avoid if possible. During your first semester at school you may be stuck with teachers that you don't favor much but it's okay because you were not forewarned. Some universities will allow you to view the rankings of college professors. They are ranked by college students and can be a determining factor in whether or not you want to enroll in that teacher's class. There is also a website called ratemyprofessors.com, it is a website that allows you to find out ratings of professors by students. All the professors may not be listed on this site, so if the professor in question is not listed, cross your fingers and hope that you chose a good one.

DROP AND ADD

In high school, did you ever have a teacher that you thought was being hard on you for no reason and you just wished you could vanish from their class roster? Well, in college you can. So, if it just so happens that you enrolled in a class with a professor that seems to specialize in mental torture; you can evaporate from the roster and drop the class. The beginning of every semester is considered the "drop and add" period. This is the short time frame where students are allowed to drop a class without being penalized for doing so. Also, doing this time frame you can add on classes, hence the term, "drop and add." If you are registering for classes and you see that a class is full, don't get all gloomy just yet because there is a possibility you can register for this class during this drop/add period. You will see that there are some classes that open up during this period due to people dropping classes or getting dropped from classes for financial reasons.

Another way you might be able to enroll into that much desired academic course is to get an override into the class. Some schools offer this option, it's basically a form you fill out and have the professor sign saying that you can be in the class even though technically it's already full. Depending on your school, this form can be picked up at the Registrar's Office.

WITHDRAW

Let's say you decide to be a soldier and stay in the class with the professor that specializes in mental torture and later on in the semester you figure out that you aren't the warrior you thought you were; you can withdraw from the class. Withdrawing means that you are dropping the course and you will receive a grade of "W" when you get your transcript. This "W" will not affect your G.P.A. but most universities have a limit on how many times you can withdraw from classes. So, you might want to check your schools academic policies before you decide to withdraw from a class.

TO TRANSFER OR NOT TO TRANSFER

For some of you the college of your choice may not be the college of your dreams. Therefore you might come to the conclusion that transferring colleges may be the best thing for you to do. You can transfer colleges as much as you like, but if you ever plan on graduating you might not want to transfer colleges that much. Some colleges require that you have a certain amount of credit hours before you can apply as a transfer student. When you transfer to another college all of your course credits from your previous college may not transfer with you. This can set you back a couple of semester hours and push your graduation date a tad bit further away.

When deciding on whether or not you want to transfer schools, don't let your boyfriend or your new friends be a factor because they are not the one's that will be paying back all of those student loans. You should consider the educational program you are receiving at the college you are currently enrolled in and the program offered at another institution. You wouldn't want to transfer from a university that has a school for your degree program to a university that just has a department for your degree program. An example of this would be you leaving a college that has a School of Mass Communication to a school that has a department of Mass Communication. The experience may be different when it comes down to taking classes within your major.

Another thing you might want to factor in when considering transferring schools is your experience at your current school. If your college experience is horrible and you do not feel as though you are meshing well with your college you should consider transferring. If you feel horrible your freshman year you will probably feel miserable come sophomore year and it may get worse with the years to follow. You should attend a college that makes you feel welcome and able to build up school spirit.

Another thing that you should consider when transferring is finances. I transferred from Clark Atlanta University (private university) to Georgia State University (a public university). My sole reason for transferring was financial. I went from paying to attend college; to going to college for free...and nothing beats free ninety-nine in my book. I lost some credit hours and my graduation was pushed back by a semester but my student loans were not as costly.

Offices you should know about...

1. **Registrar's Office:** This is where you can find information pertaining to the academic calendar, registration calendar, admissions, and other important class related forms.
2. **Student Accounts:** An office that you will probably frequent often because they handle the distribution of refund checks and they also deal with tuition and fees.
3. **Financial Aid Office:** This is where you can get on the right path to finance your college education through government assisted loans, grants, scholarships, and any other financial contribution.
4. **Academic Advisement Office:** The people that work in this office can help guide you academically to graduate on time.

5. **Career Services:** You can find out about internships, resume writing, interviewing tips, and other career related information.

6. **Professor's Office:** It never hurts to get to know your professor, especially for reasons mentioned in this chapter.

CLASSROOM ETIQUETTE

*D*epending on your high school and the classroom rules they set for you; the college classroom may be a different experience. It is a different experience that will give you more classroom freedom. You may no longer have to smuggle food into class like its some type of illegal contraband nor may you have to raise your hand and ask for permission to go to the restroom; but let's be an adult about the situation.

FOOD

As far as food is concerned, most universities won't mind if you bring McDonald's to class. Now remember that each professor sets their own classroom rules, so you might not be able to bring food into all of your classes. With this new found freedom of bringing food to class, please be mindful of your other classmates. I suggest that you avoid bringing in food with onions, tuna, or anything drenched in vinegar because the smell can irritate your classmates. Not that you probably care or anything, but it is just common courtesy.

CELL PHONES

A more major offense is cell phones; please remember to silence your cell phones in class. The reason for silencing your cell phone is obvious, it's so you won't be rude and entertain the class with your ringtones. What better way to interrupt your class of one hundred plus students than with your ringtone musical. Let it be known that vibrate mode is not the new silent mode. Nobody wants to hear what sounds like bass coming out of your purse during class. If you decide that you want to text message whomever during class, silent mode is the best because there is little to no distractions when you receive your text messages. Even though text messaging during a lecture is clearly rude to the professor; but that's neither here nor there.

SEATING

With the seating, I doubt your professor would entertain the thought of giving out assigned seating. You may notice that once you enter a small classroom where you sit the first week of class may be where you sit the remainder of the semester. Funny how that works out, but you will probably notice the faces of the people that sit in front of you, beside you, and behind you because they will probably sit there throughout the semester. There might come a day when you go to sit down in class and you think, "Dag, she is sitting in my seat." In all actuality that is not your seat and you just need to sit your front row sitting behind down in the second row.

If you have come to the realization that you have a weak bladder try sitting close to the door. Therefore, when you leave the classroom you won't be a nuisance to people trying to take notes off the board. If you decide to take a restroom break and your professor is lecturing behind a desk do not walk behind the desk nearest the professor, this is rude on so many levels; just swiftly walk in front of the desk.

ATTENDANCE

For some of you, attendance will factor into your final grade while some professors could care less if you come to class. It is solely up to you to get up and mosey on down to class. If written in the class syllabi, you can be dropped a whole letter grade for missing too many days of class. My junior year in college, I missed one class so much that instead of getting the "A" that I earned through my hard work, I received a "B" because of my absences from class. Here I am, being the reason why the class curve on the mid-term exam was the bare minimal because I scored a "99" out of "100" on my mid-term. I finished the class with a "B" because of something as silly as my attendance to class. I'm going to need for you to learn from my lack luster class attendance and go to class!

On a side note about professors...If you want to give your sob story to your professor about why you missed the last class and didn't turn in your term paper, (your dog died for the third time this semester) e-mail it to your professor or if you want to show your professor your sorrow in the form of raw emotion; wait until after the class is over to put on your Oscar worthy performance.

BE PROMPT

There are no school bells that ring for the ending of one class and the beginning of another class. I doubt that you will be given a detention slip if you arrive to class late in college. So, you should make it a habit to be on time for class; since you are an adult now. With this being said, promptness is a life lesson that you should learn while in college.

During my freshman year of college, I had an English professor that was adamant about promptness in his class. The class started at 10:00 a.m. and at 10:01 a.m. the door to the classroom was closed and locked. If you arrived to the class door after 10:00 a.m. you were absent because he was not about to unlock the door for any late-comers. I'm pretty sure while you are in college you will master the art of making it to the club so you can get in free before 12:00 a.m. Let's apply that same determination to making it to class before it starts.

If your class only lasts fifty minutes, what is the point of showing up to class twenty minutes late? It simply makes no sense and there is nothing cool about being fashionably late to class. Basically, if you are over twenty minutes late to a fifty minute class why bother showing up because you will be a distraction to the class. But, if you are the little engine that could and are determined to go to class no matter how late take the closest seat to the door. If you are late and a group is giving their group presentation, be courteous and wait for them to finish their presentation before entering into the classroom. Some college freshmen don't know this, so I know you would rather me tell you rather than your college professor tell you in front of the whole class.

*P*retty much with the whole class etiquette deal be respectful of other people around you, your class, and your professor. There is no reason to be a nuisance in class with your cell phone constantly vibrating, your vinegar drenched food or with your late class arrival disruptions. You need to set yourself on the path to graduation and showing up to class will get you halfway there and passing those exams will complete your journey...but I mentioned that earlier.

Things to consider...

- Make sure you have a clear mind while in class so that you can absorb the professor's lecture.
- Be respectful of those around you and do not smirk at your classmates comments...let's be mature about the situation.
- There is no assigned seating so if you know that you need to go to the restroom every five minutes, please sit at the seat closest to the door.
- If you are unable to attend class for some unforeseen reason, make sure that you have a friend in class that can sign your name on the class roll if needed.
- Try not to text anyone during class because you are there to learn and not forward ten of your friends a message so that you do not have bad luck for the next ten years.

GET ORGANIZED

On the first day of class in college, your professors should give you a syllabus that will outline the whole semester. That is usually their only reminder of anything that will be due in their class during the semester. Your syllabi usually explains the grading scale, so you should be able to do the math and figure out what you need to make on your final exam to get at least a "B" in the class. Most syllabi's are tentative which means the professor has the right to change it throughout the semester however they see fit.

In high school your overall grade was probably based off of homework, papers, projects, quizzes, tests, and extra credit. This made it easy because if you hardly ever did your homework but excelled in everything else, your overall grade wasn't affected because of your lack of homework enthusiasm. Your organizational skills did not have to be on point because your teachers were always willing to supply you with the worksheet that you lost and was due yesterday.

In college, your organizational skills have to be on point because your overall grade may be comprised of four exams...and that's it. So if you totally fail the first exam (because you forgot about the exam date), you might want to just get out of the class all together if you want to get an "A" out of the class. Some college courses factor in more things depending on the class, but exams usually weigh heavy and group projects and papers are generally factored in also. Regardless of how your grades are distributed in college, it is your responsibility to keep up with your academic progress.

DAILY ORGANIZER

Ladies, you should seriously invest in an organizer with a daily planner. Make sure your planner has a lot of writing space because you may be writing down a lot of stuff. I recommend that once you get your syllabi, mark up your planner with due dates for papers, projects, exams, quizzes, and group presentations.

When marking up your planner with all your courses due dates, try using different colored pens for each class. This should make it easier to differentiate the due dates of all of your courses in your planner. For example, you could use a red pen for history, a green pen for math and so forth and so on. You should also set a day to start studying for an exam or to start writing a paper. This can be your academic to-do list and can be helpful when trying to stay on track so you can throw some "A's" on your transcript.

NOTEBOOK/FOLDERS

The days of the thick notebook that comes with the pencil and cell phone compartments are gone. Please do not play yourself because it is not that serious for you to be carrying one thick notebook around campus everyday for all of your classes. I recommend that you either get different colored folders or different colored notebooks. I personally used different colored folders because in actuality, all I had in my folders were my notes and some clean sheets of paper. I stored all of my graded papers, previous notes, and exams in a portfolio with dividers for safe keeping.

On a side note, make sure you keep track of your graded material during the whole semester. Professors are human and sometimes make human mistakes and they could mistakenly type in the wrong numerical grade for an exam and it could throw off your overall grade. Unless you have proof that your grade for an exam was entered incorrectly, you might be stuck with that below average grade on your transcript.

BOOKBAG/TOTE

With staying organized you should make sure you have everything you need for class in a bookbag or a tote. If you do decide to carry a bookbag, please be an adult about the situation and get one that is befitting of your age group. If you are refusing to embrace your new found sense of womanhood, you might be carrying a cartoon character bookbag; trust me I saw this foolishness when I was in college. I sometimes catch myself watching cartoons when I'm flipping through channels, but I will be darned if I am caught wearing anything that is made for a five year old child.

Some girls opt to just get a shoulder tote bag that is big enough to carry their folders and a book or two. It can become like an all-in-one purse and academic shoulder tote. Hey, it can save you space at your desk and it looks great at the same time. Just go for what you like and makes you feel comfortable because all-in-all you're just carrying your books.

Academic Quick Tips...

- Invest in a big calendar that can hang somewhere in your dorm room and mark it up with all of your class due dates.
- Be consistent in studying.

- Break up your big tasks into smaller tasks; for instance, if you have a twelve page paper to write, try writing three pages at a time instead of trying to write the whole paper in one day.
- Reward yourself when you get an amazing grade on an assignment or exam.
- Keep your study materials in the same location and not on the floor under your bed.
- No procrastination; because procrastination and graduation do not go hand-in-hand.
- Get your must needed rest before an exam.
- Set academic goals for yourself in the beginning of the semester.

TRYING TO MAKE A DOLLAR
OUT OF 15¢

For some of you the only money you have managed is your weekly allowance, and that was well spent by Sunday if given to you on Saturday. In college, depending on your financial situation, you might be given somewhat of an allowance once a semester. This "allowance" is called a refund check; it's a portion of the money that is loaned to you when you take out student loans. You will come to know that the beginning of each semester is the best part because that is typically the time that refund checks are distributed. While I was in college I received a refund check every semester, so the beginning of each semester was like my birthday. You should check with an advisor in the Student Accounts Office to see if you will receive a refund check and if so, when will it be given to you.

THE REFUND CHECK

At times this refund check can be up to three thousand dollars or more, depending on how big of a loan you decided to take out. Before you go out and ball till you fall, remember this one thing: "This is borrowed money." So, don't forget that you have to pay it back after you graduate from college. Whatever the amount of money you receive from your refund check, you have to make it stretch for at least four months. This sounds really easy right…wrong! Trust me, when you have over three thousand dollars sitting in your bank account that Chanel bag at Saks Fifth Avenue will look really tempting.

You have to learn how to manage your money so you don't live outside of your means and live like you have big things poppin' because in all actuality…you don't. Its okay to splurge on an item but make sure that splurge is not going to have you eating Ramon Noodles for breakfast, lunch, and dinner everyday because that pair of Yves Saint Laurent pumps has you close to broke.

CREDIT CARDS

Credit card companies know that college students are typically broke and like free stuff, so some credit card companies solicit free food or other whatnots for you to apply for a credit card. When I was in college, a credit card company was giving away whole boxes of pizza to get people to apply for a credit card. Please do not get tempted by the freebies that these credit card companies give out. The real exchanges for those freebies are high interest rates and finance charges on the credit cards; now does that sound like an even exchange?

Let's be realistic about the situation, if you have no job how in the world are you going to pay a credit card bill? Oh, you might be thinking "I will just pay off my credit card bill with some of the money from my refund check; I just want to establish some credit." Boo you for thinking that, the credit line (max amount of money) for the credit card is typically more than the amount of your refund check and once you start swiping that plastic it's a wrap because that credit card will be maxed out in no time.

The credit line for a broke college student without bad or no credit can be up to $5,000 or more depending on the credit card company. One thing you can do is request that the credit card company lowers your credit line so won't have the chance to max out a $5,000 credit card. You can try to lower it to something more reasonable like $500 or an amount that is manageable for you. Please know that credit cards are not always good for "emergencies" because your emergency may turn into an "I need a dress for the homecoming dance." I'm pretty sure that is not the type of emergency you had in mind when you applied for that credit card.

It is so easy to max out a credit card when you have no money management skills whatsoever. If you just got to have a credit card, I recommend that you pay it off at the end of each month or within three months. I suggest that you pay your bills online at least two business days before it's due. You should also frequently check the due dates for your bills because credit card companies are known for changing due dates and charging late fees. You shouldn't wait until the day a bill is due to pay it, because some credit card companies will consider it late if you do not pay it by a certain time; so after 12:00 p.m. it may be considered a late payment. Make sure that you pay more than the minimum payment because paying $15.00 a month on a credit card that has a bill of $5,000 will get you no where in terms of paying it off. For some of you, your parents will lend you their personal credit cards for your "emergencies." Well, I just thought that I would inform you that your parents will see all of the charges you made on their credit card bill. So, when you go on your mini "emergency" wardrobe shopping spree; your parents will soon know all about it.

BANK ACCOUNTS

I suggest that before you leave for college you open up a bank account. This will be easier for your parents to transfer funds into your account when you have used your debit card a bit too much and now your funds are running low. For some of you college will be the first time you will make use of a debit card. Debit cards are great because instead of carrying around cash, you can carry around a plastic card. The bad part is unlike cash; you can't look at your debit card and see how much money you have. On a side note; just to be safe you should always make it a point to keep cash on you because every place you go will not be debit card friendly and they will only allow cash purchases.

With a debit card there are repercussions if you are somewhat reckless and overspend the amount of money you have in your bank account (insufficient funds)…the bank will fine you. This fine is called an overdraft; this is not something you want to get used to having. These fines can be $30 per time you use your card when your account is overdrawn. So, let's say you have $15 dollars in your account and within a day you spend $20 dollars for a mani-pedi, $40 dollars on a shirt, and then you spend $35 dollars on groceries. The bank will slap you with an overdrawn amount of $170. You many be wondering, "How did she come up with $170?"

Well, let me break it down for you:

    $20.00 (mani-pedi)
    $40.00 (shirt)
    +$35.00 (groceries)
    $95.00 (expenses for the day)
    - $15.00 (money you had in your account)
    $80.00 (insufficient funds)

+ $30.00 (overdraft charge for the mani-pedi)

+$30.00 (overdraft charge for shirt)

+$30.00 (overdraft charge for groceries)

$170.00 (total charge for account overdraft)

Banks love irresponsible people because that service charge for over drafting an account is more money for them. To prevent this from being the financial story of your life, you might want to consider keeping a checkbook nearby at all times. Some of you might not write checks; banks offer a small booklet that you can use to keep up with your debit transactions. You will soon find out that all companies do not withdraw funds out of your account the same day a transaction is made. So, just because you go out and get a manicure and pedicure, don't assume that the money has already been taken out of your account. This is when your booklet comes in handy and you can just jot down your financial transactions and you should be safe from that almighty overdraft fine.

TRACK YOUR EXPENSES

With banking you should regularly review your bank statements. Since you are probably not living at home anymore, I would recommend that you check your bank statements over the internet. Therefore you can make sure there are no fraudulent charges on your account. When you are reviewing your statement you should track your spending habits and see where you are spending most of your money. If those chimichangas at your favorite Mexican restaurant are sucking your account dry, you might want to allot a certain amount of money for it a month.

I recommend that every month you allot funds for all of your future necessities, and try to stick with it so you won't find yourself broke. If you can't find a way to break down your spending into groups (clothing, food, entertainment) just give yourself a spending limit for the month… or better yet the week. Also, never give out your PIN number to anyone; this is wrong on so many levels. You don't want to have to call the bank to report fraudulent charges made by your roommate because you thought it would be a smart idea to let her take your debit card to put gas in her car…and in return she put gas in her car, food in her belly, and some new clothes on her back.

Money Talks…

- Every time you receive a pay check make sure you pay yourself first and put a portion of your check into a savings account.
- Keep track of your spending with a check book or a debit card book.
- Track your monthly expenses and make sure you are making more than you are spending.
- Check your online banking regularly to check for fraudulent charges.
- The best way to stop using a credit card is to cut it up.
- If you have bills, pay them before the due date and not on the due date unless you want to be hit with late charges.
- Check your credit rating with the credit bureaus; Eperian, Exquifax, and TransUnion to ensure that there is no credit card fraud on your credit.
- Set financial goals for your savings account; try setting monthly goals for how much money you want to put in your savings so it will make it easier to reach your goal.
- If you know that you are going to college out of state or that you are the traveling type. Try buying your plane tickets way

in advance or check to see if they have any student rates that may allow you to fly standby.

- Shop with coupons, especially when grocery shopping. When shopping at stores that print coupons on the back or bottom of the receipt, make sure you use these as well.

- Consider buying your groceries in bulk at places like Sam's or Costco Wholesale for items that do not expire within the month; like toilet tissue and paper towels since you can never have too many rolls.

JOBS

ypically, college freshmen do not have jobs during their first year of school. This is usually because you are just getting used to managing your own time and adjusting to being in college. For you ladies that manage to fly by your freshman year without a boss to get on your nerves, congratulations! But since you are without a job, please go back and re-read the last chapter. But for others of you, if you don't work; you don't eat. So why not get a job that fits your personality or at least a job where you can work and have fun at the same time.

There are many different avenues college students generally take when finding a job. The typical job for college students are part-time jobs because the hours aren't that demanding and the pay is just enough to get you through your college life. These typical jobs are in department stores, boutiques, restaurants, and any company that has flexible part-time hours. If you don't have transportation to get off campus, you might opt to find a job on campus. You could get a work-study job on campus or you could get a job that's around your college campus. This can be very convenient because you can get off work and be seated in class fifteen minutes later!

I had several jobs while I was in college that were a pain; I worked at a restaurant, a department store, and a clothing store. None of these jobs were good for me because of the work, I just didn't enjoy myself while I was working so I would quit within weeks. The restaurant hours weren't the best for me and the commission I received from the department store was a waste of my time when added to the amount of money I made an hour. The job that stuck with me was my job as a nanny. It was the perfect college job for me because I had down time; depending on the families' schedule for the week. I picked the kids up from school, helped them with their homework and fed them. Other than that, I pretty much studied, typed my papers, and did whatever else was needed for my classes while I was at work. I was also able to take part in an internship while I was a nanny. During the holidays and the summer, I traveled with the family I worked for. So this job was awesome to say the least and I managed to create my work schedule around my class schedule.

For those of you that have to get a job make sure it works out for you. Make sure that your job does not interfere with your school schedule. Don't plan your classes around your job schedule; choose a job schedule that works around your classes. I know that sounds like something a motivational speaker would say, but it's true. Pick the hours that will allow you to study and still maintain something of a social life. If your boss is being a pain and acts like you breathe, eat, and sleep thinking about work, QUIT! But before you quit, make sure you put in your two week notice. You should make it a habit of submitting a two weeks notice so that you don't end your job on bad terms; especially if you need them as a reference for another job. Remember this is a college job, not your professional career. Managers know that college students come and go and are always willing to hire more college students.

THE COLLEGE HUSTLE

Now, when I say the word "hustle," I don't mean a dope boy in the trap kind of hustle. I don't condone any illegal activities to finance your college education. If it's ever that serious, take out a college loan in your name or just have a yard sale. The word "hustle" in the tense that I'm using means getting paid off of a talent. Now ladies, I know that you are probably thinking, "What is my talent?" It's whatever that one thing is that people are constantly asking you to do for them…do it but add a price to it. For those of you that don't feel that talented, just think about the needs of your potential college clients. Your college hustle can be something that can put a couple of extra dollars in your pocket if you don't have a job. But, don't expect your hustle to have you popping bottles in the club quite yet.

Ladies, if you know how to sew or glue in hair extensions you should have all the chicks on your hall with hair extensions down to the floor. Just make sure to tell your clients in advance that you are not licensed to do hair professionally; this may save you a trip to court. The hair game in college can bring in a good source of revenue if you are good and go to a college with a lot of chicks that wear hair extensions daily. Just make sure you avoid doing anything that has the possibility of making all the hair on your clients head fall out. You don't want to be the chick known for making people gradually go bald.

If you can braid but aren't good with extensions, needle, and thread; consider braiding hair. While you are in college you will encounter males that refuse to give up the braids or locks, which can be a plus for you. Make sure when braiding their hair you pick a public place or a place where you feel comfortable just in case you are questionable about your male client. Your college hustle can be as simple as arching eyebrows or doing nails and you can charge as little as ten dollars per client; think about it, that's ten more dollars in your pocket than you had when you woke up in the morning.

Basically, your college hustle should be something that takes little to no money to put in but you can get money out of it. Listen to me, and listen to me closely; whatever your college hustle is, take cash up front!!! I know you don't want to seem like you don't trust your clients (remember their borderline broke) but the last thing you want to do is finish providing your services to your client and they're fifteen dollars short. Also, don't take checks because for some reason people do not feel any shame in writing bad checks. Grown people with careers write bad checks so you already know college students with checkbooks and no jobs are capable of doing the same thing.

MISSING HOME

*S*ome of you haven't been away from home longer than a weekend. So, college is a big step away from home especially if you are attending school in another state across the country. During the first couple of weeks when you are just getting adjusted to being away from your family, you may feel lonely or out of place. You have to give yourself time to adjust to college life. Trust me; it is not an overnight adjustment especially when you are far away from home living in a building with complete strangers. Instead of giving up and packing up your bags, occupy your time getting familiar with the campus or go to events that are being held on campus.

Typically the first couple of weeks of school are filled with many different activities for students to partake in. The best way to become somewhat social is to attend these events and invite your roommate or someone you know on campus to come with you. Once you get into the collegiate spirit you will forget just how homesick you were and your college will start feeling like your home away from home.

If you feel like you are really sad and it is not normal for you to feel that down, I advise you to set up a meeting with your school's counselor. They can help you cope with your feelings and hopefully make you feel like a million bucks!

Ways to cope with homesickness...

1. Write in a journal or a diary. This can be very therapeutic and allow you to write your feelings on paper. It can also be a great way to write about your college experience; hey, you will laugh about it when you read it later on in life.

2. Photo albums full of pictures of family and friends are good to flip through when you start missing home.

3. Daily or weekly phone calls to your parents and loved ones can be reassuring during the first couple of weeks of school.

4. If the university has a club that is based off your hometown (The Georgia Club). Maybe you could join it; this can be a great way for you to make new friends.

5. Keep a shoebox full of stuff that reminds you of home so you can pull it out from time to time.

6. Ask your parents to send you care packages full of stuff you love and find comfort in. If your mom makes a killer batch of peanut brittle, have her send you some so you can eat it...in moderation.

7. Keep in contact with your friends and family back at home through social networking sites.

Dear Keesh,

    I am homesick and I am finding it hard to get used to being away from my family and friends back at home. I am very unhappy because I am three states away from my hometown and nothing here reminds me of home. I have been going home almost every other weekend and I find that I enjoy being at home better than being on campus. What should I do?

        Sincerely,
        -Ms. Melancholy

    For starters...stop going home so often. How are you going to adjust to your new life on campus if you're not giving it a chance? Going away to college is a way for you to build independence within yourself so you can navigate through life without your parents. I suggest that you get involved in campus activities so you can stop moping around thinking about how much you miss being at home. If being more active on campus doesn't shake your homesick blues you should transfer to a college closer to your home; or better yet, let your mother home school you through college.

      -Keesh

It's quite natural for there to come a time where you just feel a bit empty inside because you miss seeing familiar faces. Make sure you have someone that you can confide into when you feel this way; it can make it easier to adjust to your new college life. If you have nearby relatives or friends that live in the same town as your college, have them be a support system for you. This can create some sort of comfort zone for you since you are so far away from home. Overtime you might come to a point where you feel as though your college is your second home. Ladies, please be observant of your roommate. If you notice that your roommate is a little too down and just seems like she is depressed, tell your resident assistant so that they can help your roommate seek medical help.

ORGANIZATIONS

There are many different active organizations on college campuses that are free for you to join. You might be able to check out your college's website to see a list of the chartered school organizations. Also, some colleges allow organizations to set up booths during student orientation and during the first week of school so incoming freshmen can get an idea of what organizations they can join. Joining a campus organization is a great way for you to mix and mingle with people that have similar interests as you.

For those of you that are homesick, some colleges have organizations that are based off of hometowns. Now you can form friendships with people that grew up in the same state as you and you will have someone that might feel your pain as to why sweet tea is not served in restaurants up north. If there isn't an organization that fits your fancy, create your own. When starting up your own club make sure you check with the Student Affairs Department and go through the necessary channels to start your own club.

If you love the idea of being in an organization but don't really have the commitment to make the weekly meetings, make it a point to volunteer. You can go to the local homeless shelter and volunteer to tutor the kids that call the homeless shelter home. Let your inner humanitarian out the box and spread your love of sharing to the world. I promise, your soul will feel better in the morning! Please be mindful and know that you don't have to join every organization on campus. Be easy and join one or two for starters, especially if the organizations meet quite often during the month. I doubt that you will win an award for joining the most organizations on campus; instead you might just end up stressed out. So don't feel pressured to join every organization that you are interested in, only join as many as you can handle.

There are some organizations that aren't that easy to join; you can't just sign up and be a member. Academic organizations usually require that you have a certain grade point average to be a member. Then there are sororities; many females dream of the day when they can become a member of a Greek organization. At most college campuses, Greek organizations are a big deal and they are highly respected. Becoming a member of their organization takes a lot of commitment and determination. For a lot of Greek members, their Greek organization becomes their second family. I know some of you ladies have Greek aspirations, so I took the liberty of asking some Greek women questions that may be helpful in your quest to be apart of a Greek organization.

1. *When should a prospect show interest?*

Many of the ladies stated that you should research the Greek organization thoroughly before showing interest of any kind. You should know the history, principles, foundation, and what the organization stands for. Know your reason for being interested because wanting to join just so you can wear Greek colors and stroll at the parties isn't going to cut it. Many of these organizations focus on community service, so if you don't have an interest in providing your services to society you may want to consider joining a different organization. Once you come to the realization that you are serious about wanting to be apart of the Greek organization, you may want to confide into a friend that is already apart of the organization. Once again, I said tell a friend that is already a member. Don't seek out a friend just because they are Greek, they will know that you have ulterior motives. If you don't have any friends that are Greek, don't tell anybody because word travels on campus.

2. What should a potential prospect avoid doing socially?

One thing that was mentioned was that you should avoid being a sorority or fraternity groupie. Which means do not attend all the many events that your sorority of choice has, go to some but don't go to all. You should go to enough events so that they know who you are but don't go to all the Greek parties and skip the Greek community service events. It just makes it seem as though you are not serious about giving back to the community, but you are serious about partying. When you go to a party or two, try to be somewhat modest and don't let your inner wild child run loose because even though it's a party, they are still attentive to what is happening at the party.

3. Are Greek organizations eyes and ears open to the rumors on campus?

For the most part, many of the ladies stated that they listen to the rumors that are spread on campus...rumors typically have a kernel of truth. They don't necessarily base their judgment off of the rumors, because at the end of the day, it is a rumor. They mentioned that if anything, they may pay that person a little more attention just to see if that person is really what people make her out to be. So, ladies' be mindful of your actions on campus because it can probably be detrimental in your Greek aspirations.

4. When is an interest eligible to become a member of a sorority?

For the most part you have to have thirty academic credit hours completed (one class may equal three academic credit hours) which basically means that you may be eligible during your sophomore year of college. This may vary depending on the college you attend so you might want to check the hours needed with your college if you plan on joining a Greek organization. Being in good academic standing is a plus, because some schools require that you have at least a certain G.P.A. before you pledge. Some sororities may have a certain G.P.A. requirement that they set themselves that is typically higher than the school's required G.P.A. So, I suggest that you ladies make sure that your grades are in order.

5. What are the benefits of being apart of a Greek organization?

A lot of ladies mentioned that one major benefit of being a member of a Greek organization was the everlasting sisterhood. Many of the ladies mentioned that they grew as women because of everything they learned and through the experiences shared within their organization. One lady mentioned that her involvement with her sorority gave her a sense of belonging and she felt as though she matured as an individual throughout her college experience. She didn't feel as though she would have had such a growth of maturity if she wasn't a member of her sorority.

HOMECOMING AND SPRING BREAK

oth homecoming and spring break are big and much anticipated on most college campuses. In high school you might have won best dressed for tacky day during homecoming week and you might have gone to your grandparent's house for spring break. In college, both of these events are going to be a different experience from what you may have been familiar with for the past four years in high school.

HOMECOMING

Colleges are different and celebrate homecoming in different ways but no matter how they celebrate it, it's a big event. The events held on campus leading up to the big homecoming game is the fun that makes up homecoming week. You should definitely check and see what is happening on campus during that week and participate. Some colleges have concerts, Greek or dorm step shows, a homecoming dance, fashion shows, community events, jazz mixers, and a host of other things. During homecoming week alumni generally come back to celebrate in the festivities and the parties, and the after parties; which are abundant.

Homecoming week is what you make out of it; so don't mope around your dorm room like a hermit because there are going to be tons of things to do on campus that week.

What you may not know about homecoming week is that for some schools it is a week before mid-terms or a week after mid-terms. In the midst of all that is school spirit, there is also academic work that has to be completed. Some professors could care less about homecoming week; they are probably not going to the homecoming concert to see your favorite artist. Your professors may plan tests, exams, papers, and quizzes during that week. So, you have to make sure you balance the excitement of homecoming and the excitement of academic success.

<u>SPRING BREAK</u>

Another big thing that happens every year on college campuses is spring break. Spring break in college is different from your typical high school spring break because now you make your own decisions and you can decide to take a trip with friends to Miami or Cancun. Depending on where your school is located may depend on the hottest spot for college kids during spring break. Typically, the best place to be is the nearest popular beach or lake. If you really want to have fun during spring break take your fun overseas and get international with it.

Traveling on road trips during spring break is what makes this experience so exciting. You gather all of your closest buds, hop in a car, and take off to your future destination. When picking a destination for spring break you might consider going to the one place you know that everyone from your school will be at. My question to you is; why travel hundreds of miles to hang out with the same people you see on a daily basis?

Please take note that before you plan out your trip for spring break pump your breaks and consider the planning and commitment it takes to have a successful road trip. A lot of trips do not fall through because people don't uphold their end of the financial deal. For example: Let's say you and three of your gal pals decide to take a trip to Miami and since it is your master plan to go, you decide to put the hotel payment on your credit card. Well, once you book the hotel on your credit card you would think that all of your friends would reimburse you with their share of the cost….wrong! In some cases, one friend might pull out of the trip due to finances after you book the hotel. Now you are stuck trying to find someone to replace your flaky friend to ease the financial burden. If not you will be put in the situation where the hotel lodging fees will have to be split three ways instead of four. So, if you are the one planning the trip with your credit card I recommend that you get cash (deposit) in hand from your friends before you book anything, therefore you won't end up in that kind of a situation.

So, depending on the budget you are working with during spring break may determine what you can do. So you might want to get creative and innovative. If your finances aren't that amazing you might want to consider making great use of the natural wonders of the town that you now call home. Go out and catch a live performance at the local theatre or go to a spa and make your spring break a therapeutic one. If you have a humanitarian spirit, spend the week volunteering for different charities so you can make the best use of your free time. No matter what you decide to do during your spring break, be safe!

PLANNING FOR YOUR FUTURE

*Y*our college years are preparation for your real world experience. Your papers and exams may be replaced with presentations and deadlines. Those oh-so-exciting refund checks may be replaced with bills. Therefore, you should prepare for your future while you are in college. I am going to let you know right now that it can be a mean, mean world out there and having a bachelors degree is like saying you have shoes on your feet. Everybody and their cousins have probably received a bachelor's degree or a degree of some kind.

It might take more than a degree to land your dream job after college. You have to seem marketable to future employers and if your resume is bland, because you basically went to college and didn't join any clubs or do any internships, your job hunt is going to be just that….a hunt. There are so many other people that are just as qualified as you for any job. Therefore you have to stand out from the rest of the bunch, or know someone that knows someone that can put in a good word on your behalf.

INTERNSHIPS

Internships are the best way to gain experience in the work force. Although you typically don't get paid for an internship, the experience you gain from the internship is priceless. Some internship's can reflect what you are learning in class, which can make it easier when taking exams. Ladies, it is imperative that you apply early for internships because there may be a lot of college students applying for the same internship. Summer internships can be the hardest internships to get because majority of college students go home for the summer break and you have them to compete with.

Although the majority of internships are for college juniors and seniors, apply anyway as an incoming sophomore. The company might be so impressed with your resume that they may give you the internship. If you have the opportunity to intern with the same company for multiple semesters, the chances of you getting hired are greater than someone who just has a degree and wants a position at that company.

NETWORKING

Once you get your internship, network like crazy. If the company you are interning for is throwing a charity event and you are invited, go and get contacts from people that could benefit your future career goals. You will see that getting a job is not always about what you know, but who you know. Once you get this person's contact information send them a follow-up email and let them know that you enjoyed meeting them and inquire about any possible job openings or student programs offered within the company. If they do email you back and reference you to another person to contact, make sure you make it known who referred you. Hopefully through the chain of emails you are able to land a job. This is an example of getting a position based off of who you know and not what you know.

VOLUNTEER

Let's say that you are a freshman or sophomore in college and all the internships you look into are only reserved for college juniors and seniors. Well if this is your case you should volunteer your time within the department of interest at your college. If you know that you want to be a radio disc jockey, volunteer at your college's radio station. If you know that you want to get a job working in sports, volunteer within the sports department. This time spent learning the ins-and-outs will make you marketable for an internship when you are an upperclassman. When you apply for a job after you graduate you will have three to four years experience in your desired career. Now, if you can't get a job with all that on your resume, forget all of the companies you applied for and start your own company.

THE CAREER CENTER

When you get to school, you should find out about the career center. Once you find out where the career center is, make it a point to use the resources they offer. Their services (which are paid for through your tuition) can be very helpful when starting your job hunt process. As I have mentioned before they can assist you in enhancing your resume, cover letter, and they can also set up mock interviews with you so you can be a knock-out when you have your real interview.

Your college years are meant to prepare you for your future and it would behoove you to take advantage of all the school's resources, volunteer opportunities, and internships to prepare you for this thing called LIFE in the workforce.

RELIGION

*Y*our college years may be tough and the last thing you need to forget about is your religion. You should make it a point to never lose sight of your faith when you get to college. You might find that you are so overwhelmed with your new college experience that your faith is put on the backburner. You may find that you are putting your religion on the back burner because you don't know where your faith fits in with your new college life. But what you fail to realize is that it will probably be your faith that you will rely on when times get hectic during this time of discovery.

Trust me, there will probably come a time where you are in tears thinking that this whole college experience is overpowering; especially when you have two exams, three quizzes, and a seven page paper due all in the same week. At this moment, and many more overwhelming moments, all you really need to do is get on your knees and pray. While I was in college, I found that prayer helped calm me down when I felt weighed down with stress.

Regardless if you attend religious services weekly or not, make sure you read religious literature and let God guide your life. You must not forget that you are living your life for God and he has a purpose for you in life. Some college campuses have religious services on campus and if you can't find any scheduled religious services on campus look for one in the nearest town. Some worship centers may provide transportation from your college campus to the house of worship. Take advantage of this because there is much relief in the house of worship. If you need something more personal start your own prayer circle with some of your college friends or friends and family from back home. One thing you will come to find out if you haven't found out already is that you will find strength in prayer.

Speaking of religion and friends, I recommend that your values in your religion guide your friendships. If you know that you have high morals and values, surround yourself with people that have those same high standards. Use yourself as a vessel to minister to those close to you that might need a push in the right direction. If people see that you are highly favored by God they may want to experience that same feeling and decide to change their lives spiritually.

There are going to be many temptations while you navigate through college. If you walk by faith and not by sight you should be able to breeze through these temptations. I know this may be easier said than done because college is a new experience away from your parents or anybody that held any real authoritative role in your life. While I was in college it was hard for me at first because everything was so brand new to me. With the parties, hanging out with friends, and having no curfew whatsoever I didn't know where to start in terms of starting my new college life. Eventually I found that if I stayed on the path of God's teachings my life was less stressful and whenever I veered off of that path my life became more hectic.

I suggest that you use these four years to build yourself up spiritually and develop a personal relationship with God. This is the time where you need to discover strength in your faith. If you are reading this right now and you don't know God; get to know him as soon as possible because he is so amazing. If you think that he might be upset that you haven't been following his teachings and have fallen short of his word, he won't be because he is a merciful God. Ladies, once you discover the grace of God never forget it because life is so much more serene when you know you have God in your corner.

There is so much peace in the name of God and if you let him in your life, you will soon see that your life can be just as peaceful. All of the things you might have stressed over before will not seem like such a big deal. When God is on your side, you know that he will take care of all of your problems and supply all of your needs. So ladies, don't neglect your faith when you get to college but embrace it and grow spiritually.

LOVE & PAMPER

*N*o matter what life throws your way during your college experience, always remember to respect yourself and love yourself. This is not a time for low self-esteem; you can leave all that low self-esteem back in high school. You have to own the fact that you are a beautiful queen and you shouldn't let people try to rip you of that title. College is the time for you to appreciate everything about yourself and embrace the qualities that you were never too comfortable with. You need to go ahead and love those extra curves, love those stretch marks (you might as well, they probably aren't going anywhere any time soon), and love any imperfection you find on your body because if you don't find a way to love it, how will someone else love it.

You should muster enough love for yourself so that no one's negativity can bring you down. Just know in the back of your mind that you are in the process of fulfilling your dreams. As long as you know you are on track to accomplish your goals no one should be able to get you off of your natural high. When loving yourself you must surround yourself with people that love you just as much as you love yourself. This is not only common sense but this circle of people can motivate you and push you to strive for your dreams even when you feel like giving up. If you hang out with people that are not truly happy for your success they will try to pull you down, because at the end of the day, "misery loves company."

Loving yourself can be a mental self-confidence booster and if you take the time to reflect on your accomplishments thus far, you will see just how strong you really are. You have to have pride within yourself so that no one's words can break you. The amount of pride you have for yourself comes from within. If a day goes by and no one gives you a compliment you should not feel any less of a fabulous person. Mentally be your own motivation and compliment yourself when you know you did a great job; whether it is a good job on an exam or a good job of self-restraint for deciding not to go to a party so you could study for the exam that you aced.

Ladies, college is a time for you to find out who you really are and what you are made of. You will find out just how determined you are to succeed. If there is no one to tell you that you are destined for greatness, I am telling you now...YOU ARE DESTINED FOR GREATNESS!!! You should make it a point to tell yourself something positive everyday; believe it and own it.

<u>PAMPER</u>

Times may start getting rough and you may find that you just can't love that pubescent colony of pimples forming on your chin and you can't stop thinking about a big exam that you have next week. Well, take a deep breath and go do something you enjoy. It won't get rid of that colony of pimples but it will help relieve you of any stress and take your mind off of those pesky pimples for a second. If you are too vain to go do something in public, you can do things in your dorm room like have your own personal yoga session, read a book, listen to your favorite songs, treat yourself to your favorite sweets (in moderation), or you can relax and meditate. When meditating take the time out to notice your breaths as you inhale and exhale and clear your thoughts of negative energy. You can also try to write your thoughts in a journal (writing can be very therapeutic, trust me; I know). If you are still stressed out, have a one-on-one personal talk to God.

You may find that one day you are stressed out and you have a day to do nothing but dwell on two big exams you have coming up. Take the time out to pamper yourself and free yourself of the nerve-wrecking energy floating around you; light some scented candles, play some soft music, and relax. Maybe you can take this time to put a mask on your face or exfoliate your skin. Try giving yourself a manicure and pedicure or read a book. You should do something that can help you unwind and leave your stress behind. Here are some things you can do to help you unwind through pampering yourself.

THE PERFECT MANI/PEDI

1. Remove any old nail polish with fingernail polish remover.
2. File your nails in one direction with even strokes.
3. Put your hands in a bowl of warm water mixed with either cuticle oil or olive oil for 10 minutes.
4. Apply cuticle cream to nails and ease back cuticles with an orangewood stick wrapped in a piece of cotton (from a cotton ball).
5. Wash hands with water.
6. Apply a clear basecoat; this will prevent any tinting from darker polishes.
7. Apply polish in even strokes from the nail base to the tip of the nail.

8. You should allow at least two minutes in between each coat; try not to make each coat of nail polish too thick.

9. Once you get the desired look of your nail color, apply a top coat and let your nails dry.

THE BUBBLE BATH

When you are tired and just want to relax you should consider soaking in a bubble bath.

1. Fill the tub with warm bath water and bubbles.

2. Play some soothing music.

3. Light some scented candles so that the lighting is dim for you to relax; don't forget to turn off the lights.

4. Get in the tub, soak, and enjoy!

FACIAL MASK

Before you soak in your bubble bath you may want to consider applying a facial mask. I suggest that you pull your hair up into a high ponytail or just throw on a shower cap; just make sure your hair is out of your face. If you have bags under your eyes, you can consider placing cucumbers on your eyes to alleviate the puffiness while you have on your facial mask.

1. Clean face and pat dry.

2. Apply facial mask (read care label to see the recommended time for mask to stay on your face).

3. Rinse mask off with water and pat dry; your face should feel moisturized and have a healthy glow.

SUPPLE HANDS AND FEET

If you want to get hands and feet that are soft as a baby's bottom, all you have to do is follow these three easy steps:

1. Apply Vaseline to your hands and feet.
2. Put cotton gloves on your hands and cotton socks on your feet and go to sleep.
3. Wake up, take off your socks and gloves and now they should be soft.

EXFOLIATE YOUR FACE

If you want a face that glows you should exfoliate your skin to get rid of those dead skin cells that are hanging out on your face. Here are some great steps on how to exfoliate your skin.

1. Clean your face to get rid of any residue from make-up, lotion, or facial creams. Try to use facial cleansers and stay away from soaps because some soaps tend to dry the face out.
2. Moisten your face with water before exfoliating your skin.
3. Apply exfoliating cleanser onto your face and gently rub in circular motions, avoid the eye area because the skin around your eye area is very thin and sensitive.
4. Rinse your face with lukewarm water to remove the exfoliating cleanser.
5. Apply a moisturizer to your face.

CHICK FLICK WITH THE GIRLS

Sometimes you just need to surround yourself with people that are great to have around, like your girls. They can build your spirits up and put you back on that pedestal of fabulousness!

1. Call up your girls and tell them to stop by your dorm.
2. Make some popcorn or heat up some comfort food.
3. Pop in the movie and enjoy this time with friends.

These are just a couple of things you can do to pamper yourself when you have some down time during your hectic week filled with exams, papers, and group projects. Take time out to focus on yourself so that you can relieve any built up tension. Make sure that no matter how your life is going; always love yourself and delight yourself to some form of pampering.

BECOMING A WOMAN

$\mathcal{I}$ know that at your age it may seem far fetched to think of someone referring to you as a woman. That is, unless you are referring to yourself as a woman because you are trying to prove to someone that you are "grown." This term of being a woman may be, "You can't tell me what to do, because I am a grown woman!" This is not the kind of womanhood I want you to embrace as you mature during your college years. I want to let you know that becoming a woman is not so much a physical thing (I am 25 years old and I get mistaken for being under 25 quite frequently), but it is a mental transition.

Becoming a woman lies in going through and learning from life's ups and downs. Only a woman will see her mistakes and gain knowledge from the situation so that she does not make that same mistake again. Once you start to really experience womanhood, you will truly feel a sense of independence and accomplishment. As a woman you should value yourself and know your worth. Once you know your worth you will never settle for anything in life that is less than what you deserve. You should value yourself enough to the point where you know that you deserve the best. When I say the best, I don't mean the best in material wealth. I mean the best in the way people treat you and the level at which people respect you. What is material wealth when nobody respect's who you are as a person?

Being a woman requires that you set yourself apart from young girls mentally. Just because you are in a woman's body doesn't mean that you are mentally a woman because fighting in the club with a bottle of liquor in your hand is not a sign of a woman; but a sign of a child stuck in a woman's body. Instead of being focused on the petty things in life, like gossip, you should be focused on bettering yourself physically, mentally and spiritually. When you start to see just how much you think things through before you jump into action you might actually start thinking about your consequences.

With becoming a woman you should strive to be your own financial provider and not rely off of some dude's income to finance the things you want. With this being said, please do not grow up being an "Independent Dependent Woman." This is a woman that appears to be living an independent lifestyle but in reality she does not finance any of her belongings and she depends on someone else's income for stability. You should not go through life dating for a financial gain of any sort. Have something going for yourself in life and have your stuff together so you can be your own sole financial provider. When you are making your own money your dude can not deny you of a pair of Christian Louboutin pumps; you know why…because you can afford to buy them with your own money. If you let your dude be your sole provider, chances are great that he may feel like he owns you because he knows that you are not going to step out of line because at the end of the day, you need that guap!

In conclusion, I encourage you to be the super woman of all women. Grow and experience life and take note on how you are changing into the beautiful woman you were destined to be. Know your significance in the role you play with the people that are in your life. Inspire younger girls to be a woman like you….a woman that has a purpose in life and has real plans of living out her dreams.

Dear FAB Ladies,

    I know all of you are going to make great strides in life and benefit society. I am delighted to have had the opportunity to share my words of wisdom with you. I hope your college years will be some of the greatest years of your life. Make great friends and date a couple of cute guys along the way!!! Don't forget the lessons your parents taught you growing up, they didn't tell you some of life's lessons for you to forget about it once you set foot on campus. Also, don't forget to keep this book somewhere near so you can refer to it when needed. I really hope that this book reaches you in good faith and inspires you to achieve everything you dreamed of and more...and save you from making future freshman-like mistakes. In reading this, you have allowed me to accomplish one of my dreams in life; so for that, I thank you!

Lakisha Henderson

ACKNOWLEDGEMENTS

I would first like to thank God for the blessings that He has bestowed upon me and the blessings to come, because I know there are more to come. I would like to thank the people that encouraged me when this book was nothing more than an idea and a figment of my imagination; I love you all more than words can express.

To my Mom, Dad, Granny, Robert, and Lovely Family: Thanks for your unconditional love and for being a great support system. Most importantly thanks for always letting me know that anything is possible with hard work and dedication.

Japonica: You are my fraternal twin sister whom I've been best friends with since forever. Thanks for always being there for me and pushing me when this book seemed doubtful. You've supported all my dreams, thoughts, and endeavors; so for that, I thank you.

The Lee Family and Beloved Friends: Ms. Betty, Joy, Keva, Ms. Davis, Dania, and Tamme; thanks for showing me what it means to be a strong woman. I sincerely appreciate the knowledge you all provide me about life, that knowledge is priceless! Markeya, Taylor, Daryan, Mikayla, Tamaar, Phalon, Peyton, Mya, Dillon, Jahlon, and Khloe; thanks for constantly keeping a smile on my face and my heart warm with love.

Noonie: You are such a wonderful mentor, friend, and source of inspiration; you are probably one of the coolest dudes I know. Thanks for all of the encouraging conversations and for working with me on this book.

Kirsten, Kedrin, Nefertiti, and Ticara: You four are the kind of best friends anybody would be lucky to have. Our friendships are so authentic and generous with love. You all have been there for me with an open ear when I've needed ya'll the most. Thanks for listening to me and keeping me motivated throughout this journey.

Cameron: You've been there through it all; thanks for reading the lengthy original manuscript, giving me your honest opinions, and believing in me.

Shatila: Thank you for reading my miscellaneous writing samples and giving me your criticism-no matter how harsh or how much I argued you down.

Ashley: You have such a wonderful spirit and big things ahead of you, thanks for all of the moral support.

Christopher: Over the years that we've known each other you have been such an amazing friend. I want to thank you for all the lectures you've given me throughout these years and for the words of encouragement.

www.ingramcontent.com/pod-product-compliance
Lightning Source LLC
Chambersburg PA
CBHW061406280526
45784CB00001B/390